CRAZY QUILT ODYSSEY

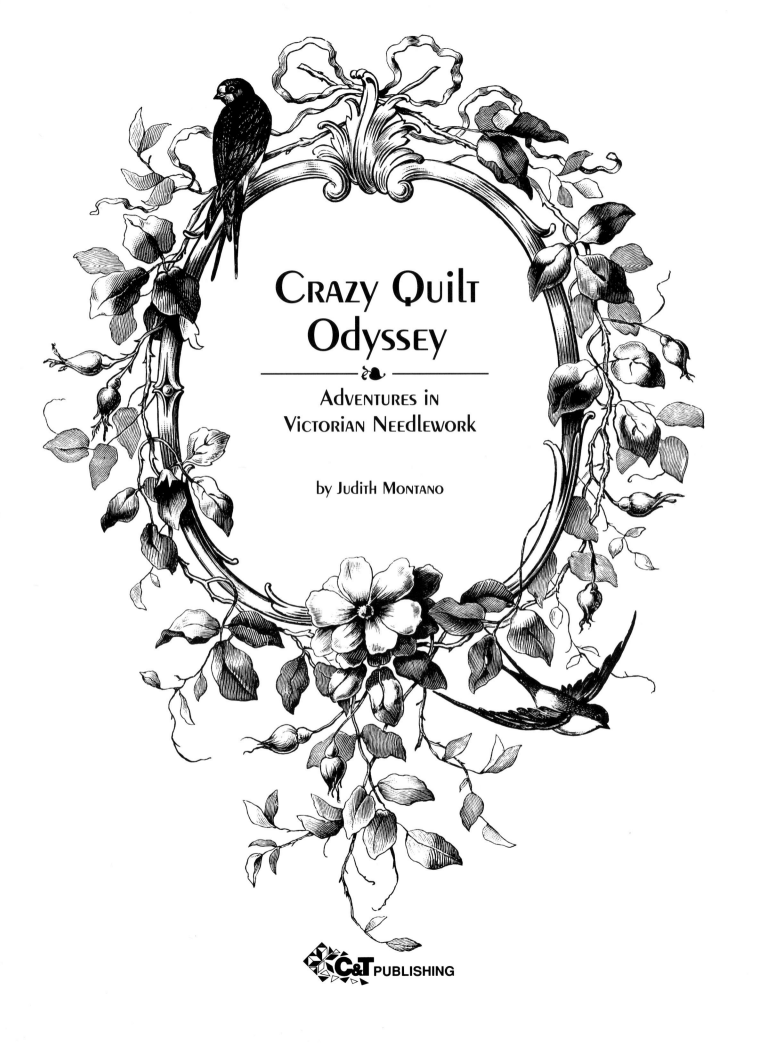

Crazy Quilt Odyssey

Adventures in
Victorian Needlework

by Judith Montano

C&T PUBLISHING

For William
My "lifetime friend forever" who
courageously opened the door to a
wondrous path and held my hand
till I could walk unaided.

Contents

Foreword

I was delighted when Judith asked me to write a foreword to this new book—it gives me the opportunity to go public with the respect and admiration I have for her work. I am a longtime admirer, and I know this book will reach a lot of people who share my feelings.

For those of you not familiar with Judith's art, an exciting and rewarding journey lies ahead! If you have already devoured her first book, taken her classes, or followed her on the lecture circuit, you will find fresh ideas and inspiration. Judith's new work is innovative and inventive, and she leads us through it with excellent color plates, well-written instructions, and dozens of illustrations.

We all honor our own traditions and heritage, for these are the bedrock and source of our creativity. Judith once again honors the tradition of Victorian crazy quilting, then shows how to translate and transform it into contemporary pieces. Traditional crazy patch was a mix of dark velvets and brocades, old ties, painted and embroidered pictures, commemorative silks, and advertising souvenirs—all held together with embroidery stitches. Judith remains true to this heritage while contributing a wonderful new mix of fabrics and embellishments. Her embroidery stitches appear complicated but are really quite easy—one of her secrets is simply to combine several for an intricate look. Punch needle, introduced in her first book, lends rich, deep texture. Perhaps her most fascinating additions are beads, buttons, and charms. All of these, combined, bring crazy patchwork into the twenty-first century.

Today, in the quilting world, we're all working toward a common goal, that of establishing quilting and its variations as a vital and indispensible part of our American heritage. Judith's contribution to this goal is invaluable. Her gift for using color and creating texture, coupled with her meticulous workmanship, is essential to inspiring and maintaining this vision.

You'll love this book. Buy it, read it, use it—and don't lend it to anybody. Make them buy their own.

—Virginia Avery

*A*cknowledgments

When I wrote *The Crazy Quilt Handbook*, I thought I had captured everything I knew about the history and techniques of this fascinating needle art. Little did I realize that four years later I would create another book on the same subject. Most amazing of all was the wondrous journey my first book provided. Like Odysseus, the fabled leader of the Greeks in the Trojan war, I found myself on a long, exciting wandering that has opened doors to new challenges, adventure, and discovery.

Not only have I met people from all over the United States and Canada in my travels, but I've broadened my horizons to Australia and Japan. In many ways, I feel like a needlework ambassador! My students and friends come from all walks of life and represent every imaginable background. They have been generous with their crafts as well as their sources—for every idea and technique I've shown them, I seem to have picked up something new in exchange! Together we've explored our need to be creative as we make objects of beauty and heirloom quality.

Through teaching I learn so much. Let a group of diverse women come together to try an exciting technique, and suddenly all the barriers come down and thoughts and ideas begin to flow—on every subject! There is something about a needle, a length of thread, and scraps of fabric that unite all women. I've discovered that needleworkers everywhere want friendship, harmony, safe and beautiful neighborhoods, freedom for their children, and a clean environment. Somehow, sharing life's successes and disappointments over a bit of stitching reveals a wondrous truth—we are all one, whether we pursue our craft from an apartment in Japan, a modest farmhouse on the Canadian prairie, an ancestral castle in Scotland, or a contemporary suburban home in the United States. Yes, I've learned all this from crazy quilting!

On the side, I've learned how to work with delicate silks, how to make an Australian seed stitch, and that rayon threads won't knot up if they are dampened first. I now know that the Canadian Indians sell the best seed beads, where to go for those special Victorian buttons, and how to make Pavlova, the national dessert of Australia. I've learned how to sit on my heels through a 5:30 A.M. Buddhist ceremony and to smile graciously while trying to swallow live, wriggling shrimp!!

To all of you who have shared this amazing journey with me, my thanks and deep appreciation. I've met you in the quilting and needlework industry and in my private life as well, and you have enriched my life enormously. Special thanks go to:

My daughter Madeleine Montano, my exotic gypsy, for her love, support, and perseverance. It is not easy living with a "creative mother." Madeleine is blessed with many talents, and I am very proud of her. She is the inspiration and model for many of my garments.

My son Jason, for his faith and pride in me. Jason is a talented musician and actor, and I value his opinions. He has always encouraged me to follow my dreams.

Gloria McKinnon of Anne's Glory Box, Newcastle, New South Wales, Australia, for having enough faith to hire me for indefinite annual tours Down Under.

Jim Huckabay, my teacher, advisor, and friend, for seeing me through arduous years of meditation, "light" work, and self-improvement.

Tetsuo Sugiya and The Kanagawa Thread Company of Tokyo, Japan, for hiring me to endorse their silk threads and ribbons. Through them I've made countless Japanese friends. I am in love with their country.

Virginia Avery, who has shown me that women can be on their own, with great style and grace. She gave me advice and hope when I needed it most.

Imelda DeGraw, Curator of Textiles at the Denver Art Museum. This feisty Irish lady hired me to be a staff aide several years ago and gave me a priceless education. She has always been a supportive friend and colleague.

My cousins, Fay Walker and Frances Lange, for always being there. Frances is the model for all my new designs, and Fay is my ever patient and helpful friend.

Tom and Carolie Hensley of C & T Publishing. They took a chance with my first book and through it all have been supportive friends and business associates.

The five very important people who became my friends during the making of this book: Bill O'Conner, for his outstanding photography and delightful personality; Candie Frankel, for all her hard work and superb editing; Diane Pedersen and Todd Hensley of C & T Publishing, for their support and encouragement; and Rose Sheifer, book designer and kindred spirit.

Ora Harlan, the matriarch of my family, who by simply living her life was unknowingly my guide and teacher.

My parents, Joyce and Allen Baker, for my interesting childhood and life on the Bar U Ranch.

Aunt Muriel, my inspiration and guiding force, and Uncle Harry, who's watching and smiling. He always believed I could do it.

Also Jenny Agnew, Jim Baker, Alice Bertling, Elizabeth Brown, Ellen Saucier-Caillouet, Dorothy Cameron, Tino Cantu, Kerrie Clark, Sally Collins, Alice Collipriest, Don and Joan Davis, Wendy Saclier, Joy Emlay, Shirley Fowlkes, Virginia Gray, Nancy Halpern, Diane Herbort, Anna Huckabay, Katsumi Inagaki, Bill Johnson, Suzuko Koseki, Yasako Kurachai, Carol Lane, Alexandra Lober, Florence Lundell, Donna McIntyre, Machiko Miyatani, Carol Moderi, Jim Morsecato, Roslyn Morton, Jane Mueller, Katie O'Keefe, Masako Ohishi, Shisiko Ono, Takae Onoyama, Normea O'Toole, Yvonne Porcella, Betty Rice, Pat Rogers, Lee Schulin, Marinda Stewart, Ruth Stonely, Donita Thiessen, Tokuko Udagawa, Jessica Walker, Jane Weingarten, Anne Whitsed, Yvonne Wilcock, Virginia Wright, "Eva" Yagino, Keiko Yoshida, and my friends at Concord Fabrics and Fairfield Corporation.

And, finally, a heartfelt thank-you to all my students. I appreciate your support and friendship. You have made this book possible.

Introduction

crazy quilt—1: a patchwork collage without a set design and assembled without batting or quilting stitches
2: jumble, hodgepodge

odyssey—1: a long wandering or voyage usually marked by many changes of fortune
2: a journey filled with notable experiences
3. an intellectual or spiritual wandering or quest

Crazy quilting is an exciting pastime, always opening doors to new designs and variations. It is the one avenue of quilting that has not been fully explored. The minute I think I have it conquered, a new technique or idea pops up and I'm off on another exciting challenge. I never have time to be bored with this amazing style of needlework, which feeds all my creative and emotional interests. It truly has led me on an odyssey from one creative adventure to the next.

At one time, I was a good quilter and won several top awards. One victory was "Best of Show" at the Texas State Fair; my Canadian pictorial quilt won over 350 Texan entries. But, somehow, the thousands of stitches I made never really satisfied all my interests. I suppose this stems from my childhood when the words "You can't do that" would ring like a trumpet of challenge in my ears. Being told to confine my fabric purchases to 100% cotton was a painful handicap, especially with all those luscious satins, silks, and polyesters tempting me from the very next aisle. Some of them even had metallic threads! They called out to the gypsy in my soul!

Childhood memories came flooding back at the sight of those exotic fabrics. From the time I could walk, I was drawn to shiny hot pink and fuchsia fabrics. Imagine my dismay at having to wear traditional tartan jumpers, Peter Pan collars, and heavy black oxfords with knee socks. I longed for a hot pink satin blouse with a purple flouncy skirt and a floral shawl. It wasn't until I was an adult that I finally realized those wishes in the form of crazy quilting.

Like most quilters, I started out with the traditional squares—produce one, then nineteen more, and you had a quilt. After the third square, I was chafing at the bit. By the twentieth square, I was comatose! I soon turned the blocks into pillows, but after forty-two pillows, I gave up.

I was ready to go back to painting when I discovered Victorian crazy quilting. It was briefly covered in our weekly quilting class, and I decided to make a stool cover. Although the hand appliqué was a bit tedious, I enjoyed the freedom of design and tremendous choice of fabrics. I turned to an embroidery book for stitch ideas and tried to cover all the seams. It was a disaster, but I was hooked!

At last, here was a technique that would let me be an artist. I could finally mix fabrics together simply because they pleased me. Lush colors in satin, silk, velvet, calico, lace, and wool—they were all there to be used like paint on a palette. No more matching points to points, keeping to quarter-inch seams, or worrying about those old dolls who stalked the quilt shows, whipping out their C-Thru® rulers to check how many quilt stitches to the inch you could do. During those years, I made every mistake possible. You could say I learned through the school of trial and error. I persevered because I knew crazy quilting was a craft that could satisfy all my interests.

As I learn new techniques, I can see my crazy quilt projects evolving from traditional to contemporary, homey to more sophisticated. The cute little tea cozy has evolved into one-of-a-kind art garments and desert landscapes complete with cactus, shrubbery, and creepy crawl-

Detail of the Semple Quilt. An Australian quilt is covered with buttons and ornaments, unusual embellishments for a quilt of the Victorian era. Owned by Anne Semple, South Yarra, Victoria, Australia. Date and maker unknown.

Photo: Margaret Rolfe

ers. My growth reflects the development throughout the quilt world, where we have seen the traditional quilt go from the bed to the body and on to the walls of galleries and museums as contemporary art pieces.

I foresee an exciting future in crazy quilting precisely because it is so versatile. It allows the creator to be historian, sentimental poet, embroiderer, painter, seamstress, and, above all, artist. For the sentimental needleworker, it can be a depository of family memorabilia—a record of births, weddings, deaths, and achievements. For the designer, it can be a chic, sophisticated evening dress, an afternoon cocktail jacket, or an array of fashion accessories. For the artist, it is a one-of-a-kind fantasy garment depicting a theme or a gallery piece that makes an artistic and personal statement.

Whatever types of crazy quilting appeal to you, I hope my book will give you the inspiration, instruction, and project ideas you need to get started. Crazy quilting appears to be timeless as it evolves from the Victorian style of yesterday to the eclectic style of today. I can hardly wait to see what tomorrow will bring! This is an invitation to join me on an fascinating journey into the creative world of crazy quilting.

Part 1: New Directions

A Crazy Quilt

They do not make them any more,
For quilts are cheaper at the store
Than woman's labor, though a wife
Men think the cheapest thing in life.
But now and then a quilt is spread
Upon a quaint old walnut bed,
A crazy quilt of those old days
That I am old enough to praise.

Some woman sewed these points and squares
Into a pattern like life's cares.
Here is a velvet that was strong,
The poplin that she wore so long,
A fragment from her daughter's dress,
Like her, a vanished loveliness;
Old patches of such things as these,
Old garments and old memories.

And what is life? A crazy quilt;
Sorrow and joy, and grace and guilt,
With here and there a square of blue
For some old happiness we knew;
And so the hand of time will take
The fragments of our lives and make,
Out of life's remnants, as they fall,
A thing of beauty, after all.

—Douglas Malloch

Yesterday, Today, Tomorrow

I am sure when a woman sits down to work on a crazy quilt gift for her child, she is not thinking, "Here, in my hands, lies my contribution to history, my link with the past and the future." But give it some thought. First she gathers the materials needed—fabrics of the latest design, a piece of China silk, polyesters in vibrant colors. She digs in her sewing basket for that daring piece of gold Lycra® spandex and satin from her daughter's prom dress. Nostalgic pieces round out the collection: the handkerchief she carried on her wedding day, a section of Uncle Bill's favorite vest, campaign ribbons from the latest presidential race. Perhaps she transfers an old family photograph to muslin.

She cuts and arranges her fabrics in a pleasing random design, taking care to show off all the sentimental pieces. Now the fun of embellishment begins. The seams are lavishly covered with embroidery stitches as well as lace and ribbons. Silk ribbon is zigzagged across the piece and secured with French knots and beads. She carefully works family birth dates in satin stitch and pens a favorite verse in a white triangle. Baubles from her college charm bracelet and buttons from her mother's dress add the last bit of sparkle. She almost hates to see the reminiscing end! Deciding her work is too valuable to make into a pillow, she takes it off to a frame shop to be padded, matted, and inserted into a shadow box frame.

Such a memory-laden piece, made by a needleworker with tender, loving care, is certain to bring great joy and pleasure. But crazy quilting is more than using different techniques and satisfying deep emotions— it is also a way of creating historical fabric documentations. Consider the interest of art or textile historians who find this piece one hundred years from now. They will know exactly what the fabric styles of the 1990s were, who was running for president, whether synthetic fibers stand the test of time, even what people wore and how they styled their hair. From the birth dates and documentation on the back, a modest family history can be constructed. All of this is derived from a simple gesture of love in the form of a crazy quilt gift. I feel that such a romantic token as this transcends all families, all countries, and all walks of life, in a way that isn't hard to understand. From a mother's gift to a family treasure to history at large, crazy quilting encompasses them all.

VICTORIAN BEGINNINGS

Crazy quilting got its start during the Victorian era. The age is named for Queen Victoria of England, a much loved figurehead whose influence spread far beyond the British Empire. She ruled from 1837 to 1901. Early in her reign, she married Prince Albert, and together they produced nine

children who, through inheritance and marriage, merged with royalty throughout the British Isles and Europe. Unfortunately, Prince Albert died at a young age, leaving Queen Victoria in perpetual mourning. She wore the trappings of widowhood the rest of her life and desperately tried to contact the departed Albert through mediums and psychics—a popular pastime with many Victorians.

Detail:
Two Japanese fans and a vase are embroidered on asymmetrical segments of a Victorian era quilt.

Who Started It?

No one knows for sure how crazy quilting started, but Oriental designs popular during the Victorian era are a likely influence. At the 1876 Centennial Exposition held in Philadelphia, Americans lined up for blocks just to view the Japanese pavilion. At the entrance, each visitor passed a screen showing a Japanese priest in a kimono walking down a sidewalk of irregularly shaped stones. The asymmetrical design of this paved sidewalk was very beautiful and delicate. Many historians believe that American women tried to duplicate the look with silks, velvets, and cottons. Another possible inspiration is the "cracked ice" glaze appearing on Oriental pottery.

Queen Victoria was a compulsive collector of "stuff," from memorabilia of Albert, to flora and fauna under glass to clothing to furniture. Her overdone style was copied by her admiring subjects, who filled their homes with heavy, overstuffed furniture, plush fabrics covering windows and walls, and knickknacks and mementos. The burden of home decor and fashion fell heavily on Victorian women. They forced their bodies into tight corsets, adding bustles, petticoats, and heavy, cumbersome dresses. Because of the lack of birth control, average-sized families had twelve children. Women were without equal rights yet were expected to present well-run, efficient households.

A woman's work was made somewhat easier by mass-manufactured goods. As the industrial age made necessities and luxuries more readily available to the lower and middle classes, they were able to move upward both economically and socially.

Leisure time—the ultimate luxury—was associated with the wealthy upper class. If the aspiring Victorian man could provide leisure time for his family, it was proof of his success and prosperity.

This produced a double-edged sword for the over-worked Victorian housewife, because the upper class symbol of leisure time was needlework. In order for the master of the house to present his wife as a lady of leisure, she had to spend hours stitching the proof of it! Thus, the Victorian era's ornate, sentimental style saw its "flowering" in the crazy quilt, which became an essential parlour accessory laid out for all to see.

A block style crazy quilt made between 1895 and 1900. Each block shows a different geometric design.

Detail:
Addie Birtchy quilt.

While crazy quilts are historical documents, they are among the most difficult of all quilts to date. The maker may have been saving fabrics for years. Her selections might include heirlooms handed down from grandparents and other relatives, pieces purchased on various overseas trips, as well as new samples. Many crazy quilts span one hundred years in fabric age alone. To add to the confusion, names and dates commemorating births, weddings, deaths, and graduations were stitched in quilts long after the actual events took place.

Detail: A flower is painted in oils on velvet.
PHOTO COURTESY DENVER ART MUSEUM

As America's first commercial needlework craze, crazy quilting was a national phenomenon, with everyone from ladies' magazines to silk manufacturers profiting. (Though the craze lasted about twelve years, both country and city women continued the art well into the 1930s.) Patterns for crazy quilting, from embroidery stitches to actual cutting outlines, appeared in magazines and embroidery books. During the height of the frenzy, magazines were filled with advertisements for new methods and designs, and, of course, new products. Painting on velvet was very popular, and complete kits could be purchased by mail. These usually contained fabric, patterns, paints, and brushes, along with instructions. Birds, animals, flowers, and Kate Greenaway children were popular subjects.

Cigarette manufacturers produced, as giveaways, small silk ribbons (about 2" × 4") that were stamped or embroidered with pictures of popular politicians, actresses, actors, state and country emblems, and flora and fauna. Each ribbon was marked with the cigarette manufacturer's name. Cigar manufacturers, meanwhile, offered yellow silk ribbons proudly bearing their trade names. By the early 1900s, cigars were being packaged with large rectangular flannel pieces that depicted flags, Indian designs, and famous sports figures. Women were not emancipated, so of course it was not ladylike to drink or smoke, but a great many of these premiums appear in Victorian crazy quilts! In many households, no doubt, a dutiful husband sat puffing away on extra tobacco to provide the silk ribbons for his wife's latest project.

Collectable cigarette silks depicting a Canadian flag and costume, Judith, Queen of the Hebrews, Zionist national flag and anthem, actresses, a wild rose, and a monkey.

Although crazy quilting was an American phenomenon, its popularity spread to England and from there to all her strongholds, including Canada, Australia, and New Zealand. (No people are more British than the Britishers living away from home!) British crazy quilting leaned toward small items, such as tea cozies, cushions, church kneelers, and small table runners. The embroidery was exquisite, and the stitches tended to meander across the lines. Many pieces featured beautiful beading and ribbon work.

"Our American cousins pride themselves on astonishing the world in everything large and small. They have certainly done so in the way of patchwork. Their crazy scrap quilts are unique in their eccentricity of arrangement, colouring and embroidery . . ."

—*from "American Patchwork," The Queen, July 26, 1884*

This British magazine article introduced American crazy quilting to English needleworkers. Margaret Rolfe, author of *Patchwork Quilts in Australia*, credits it with helping to spark the Australian interest in crazy quilting as well. As in America, Commonwealth ladies exchanged fabrics and collected sentimental pieces for their crazy quilts. Each country added its particular flavor through regional motifs and patriotic emblems.

ONE CENTURY LATER

When I first started exploring Victorian crazy quilting, information was hard to find and I did not have a teacher to instruct me. As a result, I learned on my own. Struggling to embroider over thick seams taught me to clip out excess bulk from behind. Hours of tedious hand-appliqué led me straight to the sewing machine.

Through trial and error, I developed my own style. At first, I made traditional pieces, such as pillows and wall hangings. With each piece, I grew more confident, and slowly my work evolved into art garments and fashion accessories. I found I could express myself in a fine art form planted firmly on the foundation of traditional crazy quilt techniques. I added various techniques as I mastered them. Ribbon embroidery, punch needle, wrinkled fabrics, and burned edges began to mingle with the traditional Victorian stitches. I started to make landscapes and North American Indian spirit shields, combining the lavish richness of techniques used one hundred years ago with new approaches and materials.

I don't know how Victorian ladies felt, but I like to view crazy quilting as a painting. Just as a painter starts off with a blank canvas, I start off with a whole cloth piece. The painter squeezes out the oils and begins to brush on the colors. I lay out my fabrics and begin to stitch down colors with the sewing machine. The painter adds layer after layer of color, while I overlay laces, ribbons, embroidery, beading, buttons, and doodads. One day, I reached for a spool of silk buttonhole twist because it was the right color and discovered it was marvelous to embroider with. After teaching myself to do punch needle, I experimented by adding beads. I loved their extra glimmer and flash and tried them with embroidered seams. I continue working until I feel my piece is finished. As the different layers are added, the project takes on a depth of texture, color, and interest. Where else can you combine dyed fabrics, old campaign flags, embroidery, beading, oil painting, smocking, buttons, and more in a single project that is at once sentimental, historical, and artistic?

BACK TO THE FUTURE

As a needle art, crazy quilting allows tremendous freedom of expression. It can go from ornate, overdone Victoriana to Southwest to city chic. Yet I believe no one theme is ever completely original.

Victorian women, for example, embarked on their crazy quilting frenzy in order to "copy" asymmetrical Oriental designs. Their exuberant colors and designs attracted me, and I adapted the techniques to create contemporary art garments, jewelry, and paintings. Japanese artists working today bring us full circle as they use elements of traditional American patchwork in their crazy quilting. Tomorrow, someone will be leafing through old books, will come across my work or someone else's, and will hit on an idea—"Why not use that technique in my project . . . ?" And so it evolves. Nothing is new in this life. People may come up with unique ways of expressing an idea or its variations, but the inspiration or credit can never belong to one artist or group. If we all keep this in mind, it will open up additional avenues and help us focus on better design and new techniques.

There is no such thing as an original design. This truth comes home to haunt me time and time again! I produced many wastebasket pieces before I stumbled on the idea of starting with a fabric center with at least five angles. I was proud of myself and really thought I had come up with an original idea. Several years later, after my first book had been introduced, I was teaching and lecturing in Kansas. The packed audience listened patiently while I exuded on the brilliance of my techniques. After the lecture, an elderly woman tapped me on the shoulder, neatly ensnared my arm with the crook of her cane, and drew me off to the side of the room. "Young lady," she said, "this center piece method is nothing new! Why my great-grandmother came up with that idea long before you were born. The only difference is that she kept it to herself and you didn't!"

Florence Lundell . . .
PHOTO COURTESY
JIM SAWATSKY

. . . and the quilt she made for granddaughter Donita Thiessen.
PHOTO: BLUNKS STUDIO

As new mingles with old and the precise lines of authorship blur, our sense of sharing in history takes on new meaning. It was on a trip to Oklahoma that I first met Florence Lundell. She was on a family visit from Iowa and had come with her granddaughter, Donita Thiessen, to hear my lecture on crazy quilting. After the lecture, they came over to visit, and I was instantly taken with Florence's quiet dignity. At that time she was eighty-nine; she told me about a crazy quilt she had started in 1923 and finished in

Detail: *A parrot and a cat come to odds on a crazy quilt dated 1885.*
PHOTO COURTESY DENVER ART MUSEUM

were not interested in crazy quilting, but she enjoyed it very much, learning from her mother and grandmother.

She started the rectangle sections of her crazy quilt before 1923, when she married Roy Lundell. The fabrics were bits of family clothing, ribbons she wore as a child, a piece from her mother's wedding dress, and a swatch from her grandmother's blouse. At some point, the crazy quilt pieces were put aside, and Florence went on with her busy life. She and Roy raised two daughters, and Florence continued to do handwork when she could, often for missions or to help someone out. It wasn't until 1970 that she pulled out the old rectangles. She decided to add to them with sentimental fabrics from her scrap bag in order to make a small quilt for each of her seven granddaughters. Donita received hers in 1976.

After all these years, Florence's first love is still crazy quilting, a tradition handed down by her mother and grandmother. Florence's grandmother arrived from Sweden in 1864 after a three-month ocean crossing. Her husband was killed in a train accident on the way from New York to Chicago, immediately after getting off the boat. That left her alone, in a new country, with four children, pregnant, and unable to speak English. She settled in Chicago and took in washing for a living. She remarried a seafaring merchant, and together they survived the Chicago fire. Florence's mother, Selma Widell, sewed an 1898 Chicago World's Fair ribbon into a crazy quilt. These two women were Florence's teachers and heritage.

I'm told that after my lecture, Florence poured over my book with sketch book in hand! She then went through all her lace and bead boxes. When Florence and Roy left Oklahoma for their home in Iowa, Donita said "I'm sure she will come back with some new crazy quilting. In case you can't tell, I love my Grandmother dearly. She is a special lady to me."

Florence Lundell's story is a lovely one and is typical of so many of our grandparents. She represents the tradition and the inspiration, proving to me that crazy quilting will always be with us.

1976. The more we talked, the more I liked her, and I realized she had a wonderful story to tell.

When I wrote to Donita and asked to use Florence's quilt in my book, she wrote back with this reply:

> Enclosed are the slides you requested of my grandmother, Florence Lundell, and her crazy quilt. We were all surprised that you asked for a picture yet quite honored and proud of her. Grandma has a special place in our hearts. When I asked for her consent, Grandma's shocked response was "Oh, no!" then, "Grandpa, what do you think?" She was at the same time honored and embarrassed and not sure if she wanted her picture in a book. (It might be prideful or improper for a lady of her age.)

To me, Florence epitomizes the tradition of crazy quilting—a lovely story wrapped up in a quilt. She was born in 1901 on a farm in Iowa and started doing handwork as a child. She started out with doll clothes and soon progressed to tatting, crochet, embroidery, and crazy quilting. Other young girls

Creative Clothing

In the late 1970s, at the Houston Quilt Festival, I was thrilled to walk into my first quilted clothing class. My teacher, who shall remain nameless, stood before us in a gray smock with beige, brown, and cream lone stars precisely sewn into the yoke. She proceeded to tell us that street clothes must be ladylike and subdued—bright colors were too harsh and garish. I've never forgiven her, as all eyes turned to view my fuchsia and purple outfit!

She often comes to mind when I view beautiful free-form art-to-wear garments on the fashion runways and see the glorious color palette people now work with. I imagine having to make room for the paramedics as they rush down to revive this old teacher, still regaled in her quilt block, ladylike smock.

The freedom we enjoy in fashion and interior design did not exist for our parents and grandparents—or even always for me! My chubby legs were on display beneath the hem of my miniskirts because I didn't have the nerve to go against the fashion trend. To dress as I really wanted, in long, flowing, romantic skirts, would have meant sticking out from the crowd and drawing more attention than I cared for.

Today, as the ad says, "You've come a long way, baby!" The eclectic look is here to stay, and women are now free to explore their own unique style preferences in clothing and home furnishings. With this freedom comes independence and self-expression. It is wonderful to attend various quilt and fiber art conventions and observe the change.

I can't really say which came first, the turn toward individuality or my discovery of crazy quilting. I do know I was weary of ready-to-wear clothing and wanted something different. Crazy quilting seemed to be the answer. It promised gorgeous colors, asymmetrical design, and fanciful embellishments. When it beckoned with its siren song, I was ready. There was a gypsy inside me who really wanted out!

WHAT ABOUT YOUR STYLE?

In the last few years, the quilt world has been booming with art garments, and we've been able to buy decorated clothing at shopping malls across the country. Crazy quilting is a unique way to add a personal, creative touch to your wardrobe. It lets you show off your needlework skills, document your way of life, and preserve pieces of your family history.

Purchased patterns are easily adapted to crazy quilting techniques. You can make everyday street clothes and accessories—vests, belts, purses, and jewelry—or you can design an out-of-the-ordinary garment to wear to that special art opening or dinner gala. Simple changes in color, fabric, and foundation design make crazy quilting as versatile as your imagination will allow.

ACCESSORIES

If you're busy juggling parenthood, housekeeping, and career, crazy quilting is the ideal creative pastime. It is transportable and doesn't require large blocks of uninterrupted time. Small projects such as earrings, purses, and pendants are especially easy to carry along to baseball games,

Layer upon layer of pastel fabrics, ribbons, and trims are accented with silver buttons. Created by the American designer Diane Herbort, whose work appears in national magazines and fashion shows. Modelled by Bobbi Wade.

PHOTO: DIANE HERBORT

children's ballet lessons, or the doctor's office. They also solve the problem of what to do with all those little scraps of expensive fabrics. Just store them in plastic bags and watch for unusual shapes for brooches and earrings. They could be the pièce de résistance for a new outfit!

Check out the department stores for the latest in accessories you can duplicate in crazy quilting. Tokyo quilt artist Keiko Yoshida has designed a wonderful crazy quilt belt with an attached purse (Photo 29). It serves as a sparkling piece of jewelry, and it leaves her hands free. What a great idea for those of us who are always losing our purses! In fact, any traditional needlecase or pouch takes on a new look when worn as a necklace, tied to a belt, or slung across the body as a purse.

STREET CLOTHES

Street clothes are perhaps best defined as the clothes you wear every day. Depending on your activities, the range can be quite broad—it can include your favorite sweatsuit, a denim skirt, or a shirtdress you wear out to lunch. Street clothes are typically versatile and easy to care for. Often,

favorite pieces can take you from dawn to dusk. You'll get double pleasure from a jacket that can be worn with casual slacks during the day and over a silk dress in the evening.

IDEAS AND INSPIRATION

Donna McIntyre's denim skirt (Photo 33) is an one example of crazy quilting for everyday wear. The wide band of crazy quilting along the hem is done in cotton and the seams are highlighted with floss. The matching belt ties in the back. This versatile skirt can be dressed up or down, depending on the blouse and accessories. It can go from a luncheon to an evening at the theater with style and ease.

My sweatshirt jackets with their broad sailor collars are very casual and streetworthy. I see these worn with jeans or slacks—out for grocery shopping or to a dentist appointment.

Sweatshirt jackets with crazy quilt collars and cuffs in cotton fabrics. Modelled by Jane Mueller and Madeleine Montano overlooking Castle Rock, Colorado.

Diane Herbort's vest is made of satin and moiré—very elegant and sleek. It is shown here with a silk blouse and slacks, but Diane originally paired this vest with a luscious sheer wedding gown—versatility at its utmost!

Yasako Kurachai is an artist at subtle design. Her kimono suit (Photo 31) can be worn with style and grace on many occasions, from an afternoon tea to a gala event.

GETTING STARTED

Choose your fabrics and embellishments carefully and decide early in the project exactly how you want it to perform. Will it be worn every day? Will you wash it? Will it be dressy or casual? How can you make the project adapt to both? How much wear and tear will it receive? Once all your questions have been answered, you can proceed with confidence.

If you're not ready to crazy quilt all your outfits(!), start with a versatile accessory like a belt. Depending on the fabrics used, it can go from everyday use to wild and funky. For everyday wear, stick to cotton fabrics and pearl cotton embroidery and keep the design simple. This look will blend well with denim and other cottons. To accent a special cocktail dress, try lamé, silks, velvets, metallic threads, sequins, and doodads. Not only will it serve as a belt—it becomes a piece of jewelry as well.

ART-TO-WEAR

Art-to-wear means exactly what it says—a piece of art in the form of clothing. Instead of admiring it on the gallery wall, you can wear it!

Most art-to-wear garments use fragile or expensive materials and feature lots of handwork. These garments are not washable and should be handled by a good dry cleaner. Some art-to-wear will never be cleaned and is meant only for the gallery wall or display on a dress dummy. Again, you must decide early as to what your garment will be.

IDEAS AND INSPIRATION

To create art-to-wear is to release all our secret desires. Depending on the maker, art clothing can be subtle or flamboyant. I've seen the most timid, shy quilters come forth with absolute drop-dead, sexy, trollop type dresses!

For me, the joy of expressing my thoughts and personal feelings onto the backs of size 10 runway models is a therapy all its own. I can create an Indian garment that says, "Look at me. I'm Indian and proud of it. This is my heritage." "Vision Quest" (Photos 7a and 7b) is such a garment and marks a point in my life when I went on my own personal quest.

"Putting-on-the-Ritz" (Photo 13) is a flashy little number that makes me smile every time I see it. I put crazy quilt lapels on a tuxedo jacket and added a sequin bow tie. The dress features a demure tulip skirt and a strapless crazy quilt bodice. The total outfit says "Let's go out on the town. Let's play!" I envision it at a theater or art opening.

Shirley Fowlkes expresses herself with "The Freedom Coat" (Photo 27). While going through a very painful life change, she decided to put her feelings into a long denim duster. "The Freedom Coat" is a marvelous collage of painted fabric,

Crazy quilting crosses the ocean once again! Shisiko Ono designs and sells one-of-a-kind art garments through her exclusive little Tokyo shop called Kin Keri Kin (which means "twinkle"). I met Shisiko three years ago on a teaching tour. One of her customers told her about my work and arranged for us to meet. We became immediate friends, I suppose because we "speak" the same language: art garments, embellishments, design, and so on. Now Shisiko's staff of four come to my Tokyo classes, and crazy quilting is appearing in Kin Keri Kin creations. She is truly a Tokyo treasure, only they don't know it yet! For twelve years, she has kept at her work, and I know I'll soon be able to say "I knew her when . . ."!

colorful prints, beads, turquoise, and silver. The embroidery is done with silk ribbon. This garment says "Look at me. I am a woman and I'm free!"

"Exotic Gypsy Escapade" (Photo 14) was made for my daughter Madeleine and the Fairfield/Concord Fashion Show. As I've watched my daughter grow, I've realized that she is the child I could never be—a free spirit, a gypsy at heart. In fact, for years, I've pictured her as a gypsy. This garment is my gift to her. Whenever she puts it on, a most magical transformation takes place. Right before everyone's eyes, she becomes the arrogant, exotic gypsy! Like a living costume, this garment allows her to be who she really is. It allows her freedom of expression.

"This Cowgirl is a Lady" (Photo 12) is a garment that pokes fun at the viewer. For years, people have been shocked to learn that I ride horses in rodeos and gymkhanas, taking part in speed events, barrel racing, and pole bending. They have a hard time visualizing a cowgirl who is also an artist, a mother, and a lady. So this is my Western cowgirl outfit that laughs back and says "This cowgirl is a lady." It is elegant and dressy and could be worn to any gala affair.

Art-to-wear garments are special. They can make a social or personal statement. They can be serious or just plain wild. They can poke fun or have a deep inner meaning. Some art-to-wear can be subtle enough to use as streetwear, and some are meant only to be worn by runway models or to be displayed on gallery walls.

GETTING STARTED

The art garment is a one-of-a-kind statement. Each and every piece is unique and not meant to be mass-produced. Relax and enjoy this new avenue of freedom. Let your inhibitions fall by the wayside. Crazy quilting allows you to explore, to combine unusual fabrics and threads. As you work, your garments will take on that special feel that says "creativity"!

Detail from "This Cowgirl is a Lady." Twisted ribbon cactus are highlighted with beads and shells. Shrubbery is worked in punch needle. The fabric behind one cactus has been cross-hatched with a permanent pen for added detail.

Create Your Own Look

Country—To achieve the casual, natural look of country life, use homespun, checks, plaids, wool suiting, cotton calicos, and lightweight denims. Keep the fabrics in medium intensities (dusty) to give an antique, faded aura. Tea-dye the laces and use old pearl buttons.

Southwest (top right)—The desert look of soft earth tones, spectacular sunsets, and turquoise and silver reflects a way of life as well as a region. Work the crazy quilt pieces in Indian patterns with desert colors like terra cotta, dusty pink, and sage green. Use leather and textured fabrics like Ultrasuede ® and nubby silk. Embellish the pieces with Indian fetishes, silver ornaments, and buttons from The Handswork (see Source Guide).

City Sophistication (right)—Use solid colors to give a contemporary look. Work in large geometric shapes and embroider with silk threads or ribbon in one color. Emphasize the stitch design by using a single stitch throughout the piece. Work in monochromatic or one-color schemes—white on white or black on black. Use the play of texture and shine to create interest. Highlight evening wear with embroidery and beading.

Victoriana—Re-create the antique Victorian look by using rich colors in satin, silk, and velvet (cotton velveteen handles best). Achieve the cluttered look by overlaying layers of lace and ribbons, embroidery, beading, and ornaments. Antique laces and doilies can meander across the piece. Allow the embroidery, lace, and ribbon lines to "run over" each other. Use actual antique buttons and trinkets, or re-create the look with modern brass doodads and mother-of-pearl buttons.

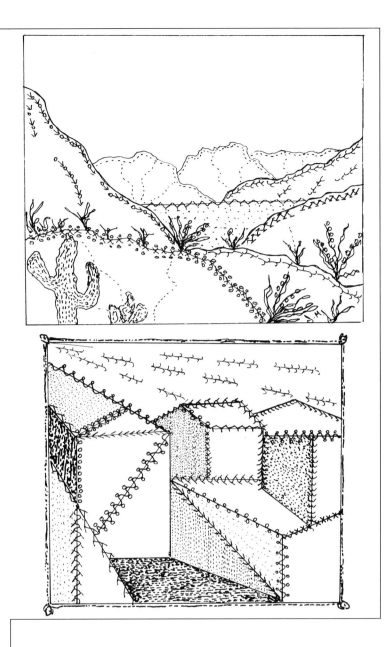

THE UNEXPECTED

Sometimes crazy quilting can take a turn to the unexpected, as the following stories show.

A Horse Called Charlie. One surprise is Charlie, a quarter horse gelding at Y.M.C.A. Camp Cullen in Trinity, Texas. Charlie is a prince of a little horse who has given over 10,000 rides to underprivileged and disabled children. His quiet dignity and gentleness affect everyone around him.

When Elizabeth Brown of Wharton, Texas, took my class five years ago, she was promptly commissioned by the owners of Camp Cullen to make Charlie a crazy quilt blanket. They wanted to honor him at a big New Year's Eve party and parade him in something special. Elizabeth plunged in, never thinking about the size of the project! Her finished blanket (Photo 36) is a beauty, a fitting tribute to this noble little horse. (Elizabeth says she'd never do it again, but I'm glad she did and so is Charlie!)

Yarmulkes, Anyone? Another surprise success got its start when I was in New York for the Statue of Liberty Quilt Show. I spent a marvelous Passover meal with Asher Paval and Priscilla Miller. As a thank-you, I made Asher a fancy silk yarmulke (a Jewish skullcap) with lots of embroidery.

A year later, my friend and former student Jane Weingarten was frantically preparing for her son Jed's Bar Mitzvah. Jane has a marvelous eye for color and design, and I jokingly told her about Asher's crazy quilt yarmulke. She was so inspired, she promptly made three for her husband and sons! Her yarmulkes (Photo 32) were the talk of the Bar Mitzvah, admired by both men and women. I was so proud of Jane's creativity and prouder still when people started to order yarmulkes from her.

Indian Fetish Pouches. As I explored the Indian ways and my own beliefs, I began to make crazy quilting fetish pouches from Ultrasuede fabric and punch needle. The Southwest Indians used fetish bags to hold small carvings of the animals they hunted for food. Each carving was made to house the animal's soul. Some fetish bags were medicine bags.

I decorated my bags with small carved fetishes and beads so that each pouch represented various animals. I soon discovered that the bags could be worn as pieces of jewelry around the neck or tied to a belt. They are made from the heart to the hand, with love and emotion. I feel very happy that my hands can express my feelings and create such a respectful tribute to the Indian way of life. Three of my fetish bags belong to art museums in Canada and the United States.

The Senior Prom. Ellen Saucier-Caillouet came into my class eight years ago at the Houston Quilt Festival. She had signed up by mistake but decided to stay and give it a try. Not only did she try, she ran with it! Soon after, she was creating and selling crazy quilt clothing and accessories. She even went so far as to make a femme fatale prom dress for her teenage daughter. When my daughter Madeleine modeled the prom dress for this book (Photo 34), the look of surprise on her brother's face said

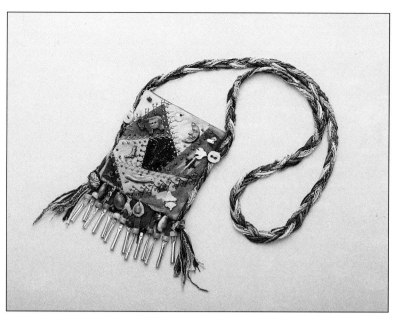

A fetish pouch made of Ultrasuede and drapery fabrics. The punch needle cactus is surrounded by bone buttons, Navajo fetishes, doodads, cowrie shells, and dance cones.

it all! Jason confided to me later that he wouldn't let his sister wear that dress on a date with a saint, let alone a teenage boy! Ellen now owns a stained glass shop in Lafayette, Louisiana, but she still has time for crazy quilting.

What Next? I've crazy quilted hats, Christmas ties, and jackets for teddy bears. My son has worn cummerbunds and bow ties that matched his date's prom dress. It's hard to control myself at times. Perhaps Sophie, my little dog, would like a crazy quilt jacket or a collar. My old Victorian sofa sure would look good in crazy quilting! Hmmmm!?

Just how far can crazy quilting craziness go? My friend Virginia Wright of Norfolk, Virginia, truly tests the limits. She always sends me bits of inspiration, like padded butterflies and prairie points decorated with shisha mirrors. One of her first pieces was an evening bag. She combined ideas from *The Crazy Quilt Handbook* with a few of her own and instantly won first place in a local museum show! She's gone on to make whimsical crazy quilt pendants and purses (Photo 37). Every once in a while, a slide of a new project arrives. There is Mr. Fish, a soft sculpture who looks like Sir John Gielgud with a wart on his nose, and a geriatric mermaid, complete with wrinkled face, neck, and sagging breasts!

MAKING CLOTHES LOOK GOOD

DRAPEABILITY

One of the biggest problems with quilted clothing is its drapeability. A garment, quilted or not, looks much better if it drapes and flows with the body. Crazy quilting, since it is sewn on a whole cloth foundation, works against this by adding layering, warmth, and bulk. For best results, stay away from heavy fabrics and battings. I often eliminate batting altogether, and in outdoor garments, I use cotton outing (flannel) or the thinnest batt possible. Always trim out from behind the seams to reduce bulk.

REPETITION AND BALANCE

Repetition and balance are two essential parts of design. Balance can be achieved by repeating fabric color, pattern, and texture across the garment (for tips on combining these successfully, see page 45). When I design clothing, I work with crayons and paper first. A quick sketch plus some color will give me a look at the overall effect. Many times, by repeating a special motif or fabric color, the design will flow much better. Quilt designs are far more successful if they are sliced and diced into sections and applied to the garment.

ASYMMETRICAL DESIGN

Trial and error has taught me that clothing design is most successful when it is asymmetrical—in other words, when it is off-center and not full of mirror repeats. Don't "bull's-eye" a design by putting it in the middle of your back. (And don't focus on any part of your body whose virtues should remain unsung!) The eye is not easily fooled. If a design is mirrored from one side to the other, the two had better be absolutely identical or the difference will stand out as a glaring mistake.

It is far better to let the design flow over one shoulder and down across the front, spilling off on the opposite side, than to clutter the garment with designs that match exactly. When a design is asymmetrical, the eye can easily pass over any imperfections.

FIGURE IT OUT

When it comes to body type, you know best what you want to highlight and what you want to hide!

If you have a short, stocky figure, elongate the body with vertical lines and solid color. Emphasize the design around your shoulders and face. Let a solid line of color flow over the body.

Dolman sleeves are a great blessing for full figures. They cover a multitude of sins, yet drape and flow beautifully. Stay away from gathers at all

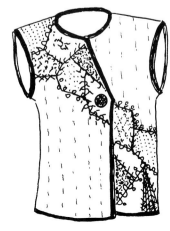

(a)

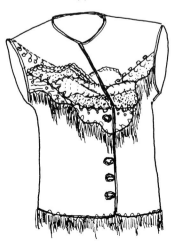

(b)

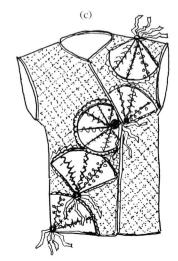

(c)

A basic vest illustrates three different asymmetrical design possibilities: a cascade of crazy patch from shoulder to waist (a), an off-center sun (no bull's-eyeing here!) (b), and fans that repeat fabrics and colors without creating mirror images (c).

RIGHT ON TARGET

I spend a great deal of time traveling now, and it is difficult to find quiet time. I also love people and I like to observe them (Mother called it staring!). Very often, at large conventions, I will don dark glasses, take along a newspaper, and go down to the hotel lobby. There I find a comfortable chair, sit back, and observe quilters.

Only in America is there such a wide diversity of regional dress. I can always spot the Californians, who wear a great profusion of color and lots of designs. A bit of the hippie era still clings to them. Ladies from the Southwest are the earth mother types with silver and turquoise, full skirts, and natural leathers. Southern ladies adorn themselves with lace, lace, and more lace. Lace collars and lace petticoats are their signature. They wear a lot of loose denim too. Preppies from the East Coast can be seen in their loafers, Peter Pan collars, and quilted jackets, usually very conservative and very neat. And so it goes.

No matter where I travel, there is one type of quilter I always see who is very near and dear to me. I'm not sure where these quilters come from,

but I think they all stem from the same quilting teacher. She really gets around, and she's been at it for about fifteen years now. Every one of her students can be identified by a string quilted vest. Each strip is exact and usually angles in a V down the back, pointing out an ample bottom. Smack in the middle of her back is a large lone star circle looking very much like a target. On the front of the vest are two smaller lone star pot holders, one precisely placed over each breast.

Now I can tell you about these quilters with great authority, for I have made the same vest, with the same pot holders, and I hasten to add, it took hours of work! For what it is worth, that quilt teacher is still out there, and I really hope that she will take a lesson in asymmetrical design. Just the slight movement of swinging one lone star up to her shoulder and letting the other fall down to the opposite side would let that design flow so that all eyes would not focus on that ample bosom! If she really decided to spring loose, she could cut that lone star on the back into two halves and set them at an angle—still the same amount of work hours, but a pleasing, flowing design is guaranteed.

---

costs, especially full gathered skirts and dresses. Believe me, you are hiding nothing behind those large muumuu type dresses! A-line and tulip-shaped skirts are far more flattering. Choose tunic tops for roominess without gathers.

The slender, willowy figure type can wear gathers and bulk. Use the design of the garment to emphasize a slender waist or draw attention to height.

USING A PATTERN

Commercial patterns are constantly changing, so if you find a good one that you might want to use for gift making, buy small, medium, and large. Look for flat surfaces and pattern pieces without darts. Think of the crazy quilting as a fabric collage that will be incorporated into the overall design.

Lay the pattern pieces to be crazy quilted onto

the whole cloth base, mark the cutting lines with a pencil, and then cut out with a 1" extra allowance. Sometimes a piece will shrink because of thread tension or a pleated seam. It is much easier to cut down than to add on. Trim the applied fabric even with the outer edge. After the crazy quilting is complete, you can cut down the base to the proper size.

A FINAL WORD

No matter what your figure type, remember that garments should drape and flow on the body to be the most flattering. A successful design pays attention to color, repetition, and balance, in both fabric and embellishments. Make sure these five elements work with and complement one another. No one element should override any of the others.

Landscape as Art

"Oh Canada—My Home and Native Land." A big title for a small pendant! Machine-sewn silk and cotton fabrics are overlaid with Victorian stitches and a punch needle tree.

My crazy quilt landscapes have evolved over the years from stilted appliqué pictorials to free-form silk collages. My art training was in oil painting, and I've always gravitated towards realism. Sometimes I work from photographs and other times I create the "real" places I've fantasized about!

THE POWER OF INFLUENCE

When I began painting with cloth, I found that three different artists were influencing my work. Each had a distinct style that I admired and envied. As I worked, I came up with my own style, learning techniques and borrowing ideas from all three.

Many quilters are familiar with Yvonne Porcella, who works in vibrant geometrics and soft subtle dyed silks. Yvonne has always inspired me to let my work evolve. When everyone was walking about in bright, geometric "Yvonne Porcella" type garments, she made a dramatic turn and began working in soft hand-dyed pastels. She has never been afraid to venture forth with a new idea.

Another influence is Nancy Halpern. Her misty, mystical pictorial quilts have always fascinated me. In them, she fuses images of her beloved Maine coastline with architectural forms. Her style is soft, muted, and subtle, reflecting her love of nature and her concern for the environment. I've studied Nancy's work at exhibits and been deeply influenced by her lectures. She's taught me to follow my own instincts and to let my crazy quilts become pictures that speak from my heart. I hope someday to fit one of her quilt show classes into my schedule.

Lee Schulin of Trinidad, Colorado, is an oil painter who specializes in Southwest landscapes with beautiful cloud formations. Sometimes, the horizon line lies at the bottom quarter of the painting, leaving a large area of Western sky. From Lee I've learned that realism did not go out with the camera (as my art professors would preach!) and that my work in fabric can be considered art.

When I work in crazy quilting, I watch my pieces evolve into pictures that are realistic yet mystical and very much my own creations. Whereas Lee uses most of her canvas for sky, I like to slice into the earth and show it as a web of traditional crazy quilting.

Two Ways to Work

FANTASY LANDSCAPES

I enjoy working fantasy landscapes the most as they range from very traditional crazy quilting to almost abstract scenery. "Never Never Land" (Photo 23) evolved from my concern for the environment. It features many types of fish and turtles all caught up in the webbing of the traditional crazy quilting. The Oriental lily pond just happened and adds a profusion of color. The Southwest desert and mountains float in the background, making a truly fantasy "Never Never Land."

"Lady Lives On" (cover and Photo 24) is a very personal piece. My daughter Madeleine is an accomplished rider and had a beautiful quarter horse mare named Lady. They were inseparable and to see them perform was beautiful. Unfortunately, Lady became very ill and after surgery did not recover. When we went to say goodbye to her, Madeleine's main concern was whether Lady would go to heaven.

"Lady Lives On" shows a lovely world filled with animal fetishes and beautiful, peaceful colors. Traditional crazy quilting forms the earth foundation, which evolves into a pictorial landscape. A beautiful horse button marks Lady's burial plot and off to the left on the hillside is a prancing mare with shiny wings on her way to heaven. The punch needle tree is reminiscent of my Canadian ranch home. Somehow, no matter how hard I try to prevent it, my pictures always take on an Oriental Southwest look!

DESIGNING FROM PHOTOGRAPHS

Landscapes can also be made from photographs. I enjoy the challenge of photography, and sometimes I happen to produce a good picture! Some photos are so memorable that I've gone a step further and reproduced them in crazy quilt landscapes. The landscapes can adorn a wooden box lid, decorate a pillow or a piece of jewelry, or simply be framed. Landscapes can commemorate a occasion or a holiday trip or capture a childhood memory or place.

I commemorated Fisher's Peak in the shape of a small wooden box lid (Photos 19a and 19b) for my aunt, Ora Harlan. Fisher's Peak is a landmark outside of Trinidad, Colorado, where Ora lived. My sister and I attended junior college in this little mining town, and Ora was our anchor, always checking up on us and cooking us wonderful fried chicken dinners. She always displayed my artwork in her home— some of it good and some of it terrible—and was always proud of me. When she turned ninety, I made this special box for her. Fisher's Peak is burned silk and the texture is made by punch needle. Each seam is covered in Victorian stitches.

"Malua Bay at Sunrise" (Photos 20a and 20b) commemorates a special morning in Australia. I was given a birthday gift of four days at a cottage that overlooked Malua Bay, a beautiful spot along a rugged coastline where dolphins come to play. It is a magical place. My version is made of silk and antique lace. The cliff is a burned shape overlaid with heavy antique lace for texture. The clouds in the sunrise sky are lines of metallic featherstitches. The foreground is worked in ribbon embroidery.

Another Australian scene suggested itself last year, as I drove along the coastline from Newcastle to Gosford in the late afternoon. A storm was coming in and the sky was vivid peach and dusty pink. I chose my best slide out of twenty to work this wonderful memory into a small porthole picture. I call it "Norah Head Beach at Sunset" (Photos 21a and 21b). The sky is dyed silk that has been detailed with acrylic paints. The foreground is a mass of French knots, featherstitches, and straight stitches for texture.

One small pendant I call "Nancy Halpern's Maine" (Photo 22b). I worked it from a slide Nancy loaned me from her lecture series. The Maine water oaks reminded me of Canada and the beautiful autumn colors. Many interesting fabrics went into this small piece. The water was made from silk scraps sent to me by Yvonne Porcella. They were left over from a quilt she made on commission for the puppeteer Jim Henson. The quilt arrived the day before he died and he never saw it. I decided to use some of the silk in my "water oaks" pendant, over-laying it with acrylic paint to create the watery surface. The river bank is a piece of silk dyed by Roslyn Morton of Brisbane, Australia. Roslyn is a very talented dye artist and a flight attendant on Ansett Australia. She gave me a bag of scraps on my last Australian trip. The oaks are worked in silk buttonhole twist and silk ribbon from Kanagawa in Tokyo, Japan. This pendant, which can be worn on the body or hung on the wall, is full of international memories.

CREATING THE LANDSCAPE

Each crazy quilt landscape begins with a sketch on paper. Photos or pictures, if used, should be sharp and clear. Try to simplify the shape of the land in your sketch. Remember, you can add details with embellishments. Once you are pleased with the sketch or pattern, transfer it to muslin and cut out ½" (12 mm) all around.

Remember always that you are painting with fabrics. Look at the pattern sketch and determine the sequence for laying down the fabric pieces. Imagine that you are traveling through the landscape from the farthest point to the foreground and lay down the farthest pieces first. Pieces with curvy burned edges will be very lightly glued in until they can be embroidered down. Others will be sewn in. I prefer working with silk because it is so manageable.

Wrinkles stay in, the colors are vibrant, and it presses under for appliqué—in other words, it stays where you place it! If the land-scape is to be matted and framed, you can use the matte as a win-dow template, laying it down as the work progresses to check for color, texture, and depth. (For step-by-step instructions, see page 50.)

The fabrics anchored into place are the foundation of the landscape scene. Like in tradi-tional crazy quilting, I stitch over every seam with Victorian em-broidery stitches. The lines of the hills and mountains that edge up to the sky need a special treat-ment if they are to look realistic. Keep the embroidery on the side of the hills and not flying up into

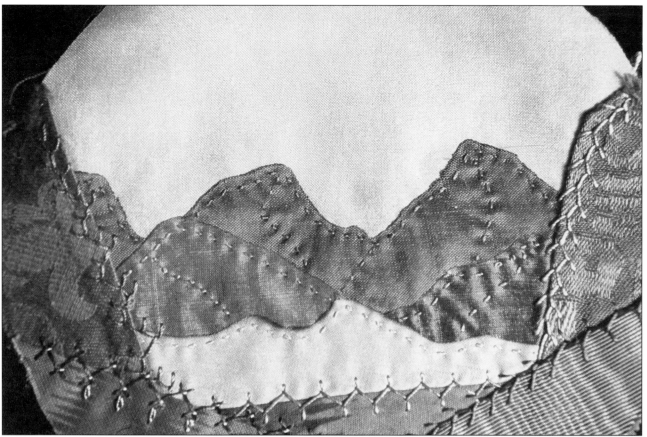

A landscape in progress. Victorian stitches and running stitches hold down foundation pieces awaiting further embellishment.

the sky. Sometimes a simple running stitch is all you need. It can act as a line drawing to give detail. If buildings are involved, lay down a shape from fabric and then embroider in the details. Use a variety of threads, ribbons, and yarns to add texture to your landscape.

Once all the seams have been decorated, I go over the piece with a textural ribbon, such as silk or spark organdy. It can be twisted and manipulated and held down with French knots or beads. Shadow and light are created by use of color, but you can increase shadow and detail with acrylic paints or permanent pens. Further texture and detail can be added with punch needle embroidery. Take extra care as you are punching through two layers.

Remember always that landscapes are creative impressions taking shape from your imagination and memories. You are the creator and the artist.

ANTIQUE CRAZY QUILTS

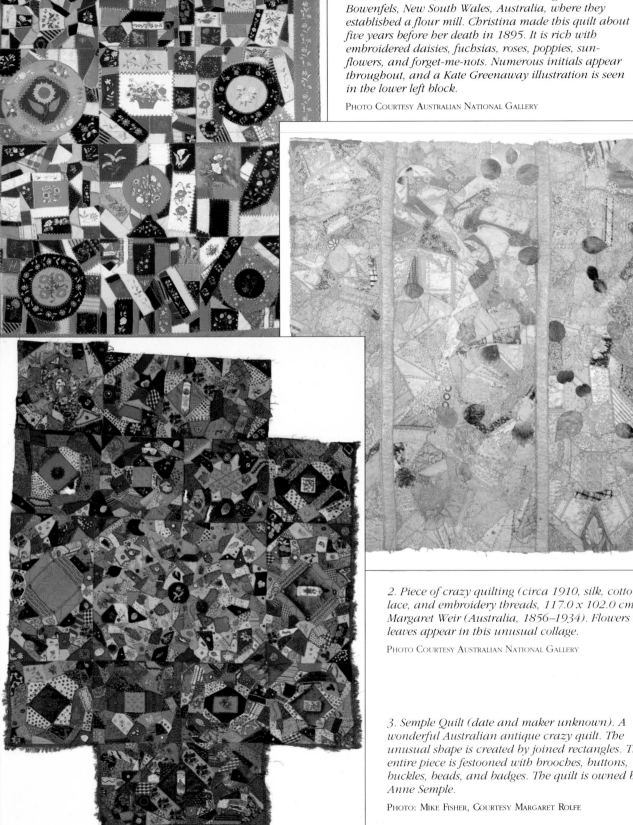

1. Australian Antique Quilt (circa 1890, silk and cotton, 181.0 x 146.0 cm) by Christina Brown. Christina Henderson was born in Scotland in 1815. In 1842, she and her husband, Andrew Brown, immigrated to Bowenfels, New South Wales, Australia, where they established a flour mill. Christina made this quilt about five years before her death in 1895. It is rich with embroidered daisies, fuchsias, roses, poppies, sunflowers, and forget-me-nots. Numerous initials appear throughout, and a Kate Greenaway illustration is seen in the lower left block.

PHOTO COURTESY AUSTRALIAN NATIONAL GALLERY

2. Piece of crazy quilting (circa 1910, silk, cotton lace, and embroidery threads, 117.0 x 102.0 cm) by Margaret Weir (Australia, 1856–1934). Flowers and leaves appear in this unusual collage.

PHOTO COURTESY AUSTRALIAN NATIONAL GALLERY

3. Semple Quilt (date and maker unknown). A wonderful Australian antique crazy quilt. The unusual shape is created by joined rectangles. The entire piece is festooned with brooches, buttons, buckles, beads, and badges. The quilt is owned by Anne Semple.

PHOTO: MIKE FISHER, COURTESY MARGARET ROLFE

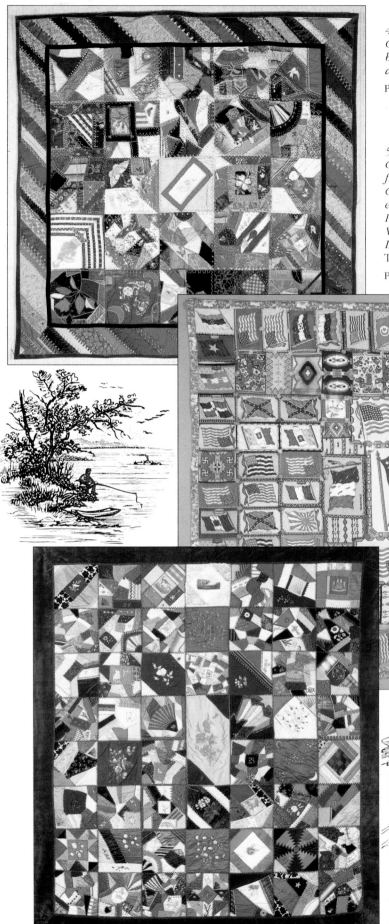

4. *American Antique Crazy Quilt (circa 1890) by Catherine Hume Simons. The quilt is made up of twenty blocks surrounded by an angled strip border. Silk, satin, and cotton fabrics were used.*

5. *American Flag Quilt (date and maker unknown). Cigar flannel quilt with floursack backing featuring flag, rug, and baseball premiums from the Sweet Corporal Tobacco Company. American flag has forty-eight stars. The swastika symbol is an original American Indian design representing North, South, East, and West. Gift of the author to the textile department of the Denver Art Museum in gratitude for its assistance with The Crazy Quilt Handbook.*

6. *Antique Crazy Quilt (circa 1885, maker unknown). Eight-inch blocks of brocades, satins, plush, and velvets with embroidery.*

JUDITH MONTANO'S ONE-OF-A-KIND ART GARMENTS, LANDSCAPES, AND INDIAN ARTIFACTS

9. "Bar U Cradle Board." An Indian baby carrier or "moss bag," as it is called in Alberta, Canada. The mother packed moss in the cradle board around the baby to act as a natural diaper. This version is made of deerskin and coyote pelt with punch needle on velvet. Gift from the author to her father, Allen Baker. Bar U is the family cattle brand.

PHOTO: STUART LANGE

7a and 7b. "Vision Quest." An Ultrasuede jacket and dress created for the 1988 Fairfield/Concord Fashion Show. The eagle on the back represents the strength or vision of the Indian culture. The tree is shown firmly "rooted" in the earth of tradition. Modelled by Madeleine Montano.

PHOTOS: BILL O'CONNER

10. Navajo Indian blouse. Punch needle takes on a sophisticated look in the shape of tiger lilies and bleeding hearts. Buttons are antique silver conchos. Modelled by Alexandra Lober.

8. A variety of fetish bags made of Ultra-suede, punch needle, and twisted ribbon. Each seam is embroidered with silk button-hole twist and embellished with buttons from The Handswork (see Source Guide), bone buttons, and Navajo fetish carvings. The tassels are decorated with feathers, pony beads, and aluminum dance cones.

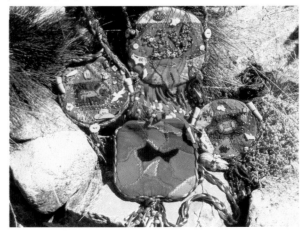

11. A hoop-shaped spirit shield echoes the unbroken circle that is so essential to the Indian beliefs. The North American Indians used such shields for spiritual protection. The author re-creates them to express her emotions, dreams, and beliefs. This interpretation combines many techniques and materials. The deerskin was a gift of the author's brother, Jim Baker. The Oriental type tree is worked in punch needle on silk noile. The crazy quilt landscape is silk with embroidery and beads. Note the bird in the sky and the buffalo skull in the foreground.

12. *"This Cowgirl is a Lady." An Ultrasuede skirt, scene vest, cocoon jacket, and purse created for the 1989 Fairfield/Concord Fashion Show. Each cactus and flower is made of twisted ribbon tacked down with beads, pearl buttons, and pucha shells. Modelled by Frances Lange.*

PHOTO: BILL O'CONNER

13. *"Putting on the Ritz." A cocktail dress with a crazy quilt bodice is topped by a velvet tuxedo jacket. A beaded satin bow tie is worn as a necklace. The jacket's rich velvet repeats in the escort's bow tie and cummerbund. Made for the Fairfield/Concord 1987 Fashion Show. Modelled by Frances Lange and Jason Montano.*

PHOTO: BILL O'CONNER

14. *"Exotic Gypsy Escapade." A fantasy outfit! Skirt of crushed velvet is topped by a crazy quilt weskit. Ultrasuede jacket is encrusted with a punch needle flower and a shower of leaves with burned edges. Coordinating accessories include a crystal pouch, Ultrasuede earrings, necklace, and headband. Made for the Fairfield/Concord 1990 Fashion Show; a gift of the author to her daughter. Modelled by Madeleine Montano.*

PHOTO: BILL O'CONNER

15. *"Australian Sands." A scene vest made of hand-dyed silks over a polished cotton body. Modelled by Alexandra Lober with her acubra hat and stock saddle.*

16. *The front and back muslin yokes for each of these vests were crazy-quilted separately, then applied to the main pattern pieces during construction. Modelled by Kerrie Clark, Madeleine Montano, and Jane Mueller in red rocks of Deer Creek Canyon near Castle Rock, Colorado.*

PHOTO: BILL O'CONNER

17. *Detachable crazy quilt collars dress up school outfits for Katie O'Keefe, Anna Huckabay, and Jessica Walker. The antique crazy quilt teddy is the fiftieth bear made by Alice Collipriest of Citrus Heights, California. The author made the red and white Christmas teddy.*

PHOTO: BILL O'CONNER

18. *"Uptown Lady." Wool and Ultrasuede coat is an adaptation of the Folkwear® Turkish Coat. The author added deep dolman sleeves and rattail ties. The half-circle purse has a fan design (see Project P-3). Modelled by Frances Lange.*

PHOTO: BILL O'CONNER

19a and 19b. "Fisher's Peak." The author spent a happy year here while attending junior college. The box was a gift to her "Aunt" Ora Harlan, the matriarch of the family, on her nineteenth birthday. Fisher's Peak overlooks the old mining town of Trinidad, Colorado.

PHOTO: BILL O'CONNER

20a and 20b. "Malua Bay at Sunrise." This special hideaway cove nestles among the craggy cliffs along the coastline of New South Wales, Australia. During a 5 a.m. walk along the beach, the author captured this spectacular sunrise on film and later commemorated the moment in a jewelry box. The cliffs are collaged antique laces with ribbon embroidery in the foreground. The sky is a wash of acrylic paints over "Porcella" silk. Antique buttons and beads add to the embellishments. Box by Tennessee Wood Crafters (see Source Guide).

*21a and 21b. "Norah Head Beach at Sunset."
A storm was coming in as the author drove
from Newcastle to Gosford along the New
South Wales, Australia, coastline. The sky
turned peachy pink, compelling her to stop
and run up the path at Norah Head Beach
with her camera. The oval picture based on
the photo has a painted sky. Burned silk
pieces are held down with straight stitches
and French knots of yarn, silk, and ribbon.*

*22a and 22b. "Nancy Halpern's Maine." A pendant
with water oaks is based on a slide taken off mid-
coast Maine, somewhere between Boothbay
and Damariscotta. Nancy Halpern uses
the slide in her lectures. It had sentimental appeal for the author because the
oak tree is common in her native
Canada. Yvonne Porcella donated
the silk scraps from a quilt she made
for Jim Henson. Roslyn Morton, a
flight attendant for Ansett Australia,
dyed the green fabric. Trees are
worked in silk buttonhole twist and
ribbon.*

23. "Never-Never Land." An imaginary scene showing a desert with a view underground. The underworld is a web of traditional crazy quilting that has ensnared fish, turtles, and frogs. The oasis above takes on an Oriental flare in a profusion of silk ribbon embroidery. As a portrayal of a desert built upon the ocean, this imaginary land shows concern for the future of our environment.

PHOTO: BILL O'CONNER

24. "Lady Lives On." The author made this picture to answer her daughter Madeleine's question, "Do animals go to heaven?" Lady was Madeleine's prize quarter horse mare who died following an illness. The underground is filled with various animal fetishes. A beautiful horse button marks Lady's burial plot, and on the left hillside is a heaven-bound horse with shiny wings. Judith Montano writes, "Animals do die, but I believe their souls go to heaven. Our pets wait for us there."

PHOTO: BILL O'CONNER

Part 2: The Basics

Here's everything you need to know to start crazy quilting, from choosing the first piece of fabric to sewing on the final button. All you have to provide is your imagination!

Choosing Your Fabrics

WHERE TO SHOP

One special beauty of crazy quilting is the variety—and quantity—of fabrics that can be used. My theory is "if it doesn't melt under the iron—use it!" This philosophy has opened up a whole new world of fabric shops and sources to me. I am constantly looking for new selections and ideas. It used to be that half a yard of a fabric was enough—now I'm up to ten yards if it's really special! I've wheedled men out of silk ties at parties, and some students in my classes feel very uncomfortable when I carry on about the beauty of their clothing (especially with scissors at close reach!). I've walked thirty blocks in the rain for a special lace, and after the discovery of couturier fabrics, I've never been quite the same! One warning I issue to all my students: Crazy quilting is addictive, and it can be costly—especially if you discover the world of couturier fabrics and silks.

When you start crazy quilting, you'll find you support all types of fabric stores. I visit my favorite shops at least once a month to see what's new.

Standard Fabric Stores. Make the local fabric and notions shop your first stop. Here you can find dress-weight cottons, polyesters, fancy fabrics, and craft items. The best buys are in the back on the bargain tables. In *The Crazy Quilt Handbook*, I urged my readers to pick up half-yard pieces for crazy quilting. I've already confessed to going well beyond the half-yard habit, so you are on your own!

Quilt Shops. If you think quilt shops carry just calico prints, look again! The range travels from big, overall exotic prints to holiday motifs to plaids. Glazed solid cottons can be used on both sides.

Drapery Fabric Stores. Home furnishing shops are one of my favorite places to shop—most of the fabric comes in 54" widths! Look for big decorator prints and drapery-weight moiré. The drapery weight is much thicker and softer than dress-weight moiré. It also drapes nicely for clothing construction and makes a good foundation for punch needle embroidery.

Thrift Shops and Garage Sales. Don't overlook secondhand sources for vintage fabrics, hankies, and ties. Most ties are silk or a synthetic jacquard weave. This means the pattern on the back is a reverse of the front, so you get two fabrics for the price of one! Ties are easy to pull apart and can be stored flat.

Couturier Shops. Last, and my favorites, are the specialists in formal, bridal, and designer fabrics. The silks, brocades, satins, and cashmeres will take away your breath as well as your money! (In my hometown, one specialty shop has a layaway plan!) I especially love working with silk. It can be used in so many ways and adds a beautiful shimmer. I realize that one hundred years from now, it may deteriorate, but it's well worth the gamble.

In the late 1800s, silk and other fabrics were produced in huge East Coast mills. Magazine ads of the period invited the public to send for small samples, choose their favorites, and place an order. It took the bookkeepers awhile to realize that the samples going out far exceeded the orders coming in—the small swatches were perfect for crazy quilting, and women were swapping them with friends! At first, manufacturers tacked on a charge to cover their costs, but the demand was so great, they soon began advertising bundles of assorted fabrics just for crazy quilting.

Decide right from the start whether your finished piece will be washed or dry-cleaned. If I plan to use a piece every day and washability is important, I "destroy" all the fabrics before I ever sew with them. Silks, satins, velvets, *everything*, goes in the washer at a high temperature. What I get out of a hot dryer is what I use! Most of my work requires long hours and is heavily embellished, so I prefer to have it dry-cleaned. Always choose a reputable cleaner. You can really impress them by asking to have your piece dipped in the morning's first solution, when it is the cleanest.

🍂 **Home Sweet Home.** You'll find one last piece of fabric right in your own sewing room. Crazy quilting is always sewn down to a whole cloth foundation piece. Choose something lightweight,

like cotton. Because the front and back are covered, you can use up a lot of old fabrics and put them to good use.

WHAT ABOUT COLOR?

I find that, no matter where I teach, color is a difficult subject for my students. My theory is that as babies we are born with basic instincts that we have to give up over the years in order to conform. Society keeps us well in tow by dictating acceptable behavior, life-styles, careers, fashions, and yes, even color choices! Each year we hear from the gurus of fashion and interior design, who tell us exactly how we should decorate our homes and bodies, and, of course, what colors we should use. In recent years, we have been inundated with color consultants who help us to decide whether we are a "winter," "spring," "summer," or "fall." The theory is a very good one,

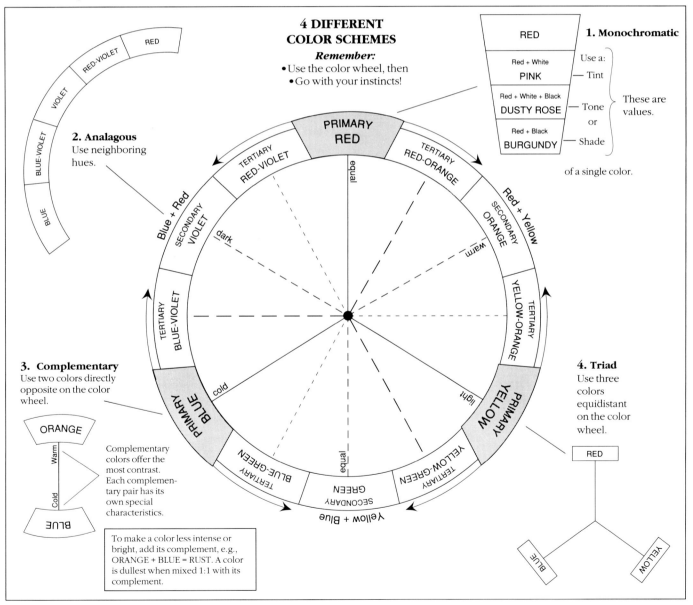

4 DIFFERENT COLOR SCHEMES

Remember:
• Use the color wheel, then
• Go with your instincts!

1. Monochromatic
Use a:
— Tint
— Tone or
— Shade
These are values.
of a single color.

RED
Red + White — PINK
Red + White + Black — DUSTY ROSE
Red + Black — BURGUNDY

2. Analagous
Use neighboring hues.

3. Complementary
Use two colors directly opposite on the color wheel.

Complementary colors offer the most contrast. Each complementary pair has its own special characteristics.

To make a color less intense or bright, add its complement, e.g., ORANGE + BLUE = RUST. A color is dullest when mixed 1:1 with its complement.

4. Triad
Use three colors equidistant on the color wheel.

but in many ways it has become a commercial ploy that some women take too seriously. There is a part of me that doesn't want to find out that fuchsia is not my color! I encourage my students to go with their instincts and to use common sense. Most people gravitate towards one color. They like it and it makes them feel good. Therefore they should wear it and enjoy!

THE COLOR WHEEL

The color wheel can help take the mystery out of color choices. The wheel shows the whole spectrum of colors arranged in a circle. In nature, the colors are grouped in four basic ways: monochromatic, analogous, complementary, and triad. Study the color wheel, then try working a combination you like with crayons or paint before cutting into your fancy fabrics.

COLOR IN FABRICS

Crazy quilting may look like a jumble of colors, but it's really a well-orchestrated piece of art. By applying a few additional principles, you can come up with many pleasing combinations.

VALUE

If you've chosen a color scheme other than monochromatic, decide what value you will work in. Value tells us how light, medium, or dark a particular color is. In fabric language, this translates to pastels, dusty shades, or jewel tones. Sticking to one value is important. If you mix the values of different hues, the finished piece will look spotty. In a jewel-tone pendant with black as a neutral, a piece of white or a dusty tone would look out of place.

DEPTH AND DISTANCE

Remember the old art adage "lights come forward and darks recede"? In a crazy quilt mountain picture, the farthest mountain would be the darkest, and as you work forward, the colors would lighten to give a feeling of depth. Use the same principle in random designs. When making a small pendant, start with a dark center. It is usually embellished with needlework, and because it is dark, the eye will immediately travel to it. The dark center recedes.

With this value	Use these neutrals
◆Pastel	White Cream Metallic Silver Metallic Gold
◆Dusty	Gray Taupe Metallic Silver Metallic Gold
◆Jewel Tone	Black Metallic Silver Metallic Gold

Dark center pieces show off needlework and embellishments on four weeping heart pendants.

The Role of Neutrals

A neutral fabric can be added to any multicolor combination without changing the basic effect. The perfect print neutral would have the chosen neutral background and two of the chosen colors in the design. Look for these!

Neutral fabrics act as a base for the colors—visualize colors floating on a lake of neutrals. The eye will travel across the patchwork in an easy movement, much the way it scans a pointillist painting. In this technique, the painter uses dots of pure color. When you stand close to the painting, you are aware of the tiny dots. When you stand back, the dots "disappear" into a harmony of color. Crazy patchwork works on the same principle. Assorted fabrics, in colors and neutrals, are cut into different shapes and arranged in a pleasing composition. The viewer notices these patches upon close examination, but from a distance, they form a lovely flow of color.

You'll want a variety of solids, prints, and textures to coordinate with your color and intensity choices. Because I work in expensive fabrics and my costs are soaring, I buy neutrals in cheaper cuts to bring down the cost of the finished piece.

Solids, Prints, and Textures

Beautiful embroidery and embellishments take hours of painstaking work, and you want to be sure that your efforts show. The secret, in both contemporary and traditional designs, lies in the crazy patch foundation. It should include a balance of solids, prints, and textures.

❦ **Solid**—Fabric that is one color only. Look for solids that can be used front and back.

❦ **Print**—Fabric that has a pattern, such as pin dot, calico, decorator florals, and plaids. The pattern can be large or small. Watch for prints that have more than one color, as they are a good buy and can be used in many projects.

❦ **Texture**—Fabric with a special feel to it. Some examples are wool, velvet, raw silk, jacquard

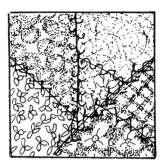

DON'T USE
prints only

DON'T USE
textures only

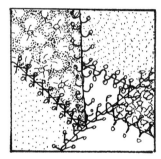

DO USE
solids, prints, and textures

weaves, and moiré. A texture can be solid or printed.

Even though crazy quilting is free-form, when it comes to fabric placement, I have a cardinal rule:

☞ *Do not put pattern against pattern.*

A piece that's "all pattern" means the stitching will not show. All textures will look heavy, and the stitches tend to get hidden in the nap and plush. Always bounce solids off of prints and textures. Bounce color off color. To harmonize with their neighbors, fabric types must complement, not match, each other.

Laying the Foundation

*I*t's time to see that wonderful pile of fabrics you've assembled come to life! You've already laid the cornerstone of your crazy quilting by working within a color scheme and choosing a variety of solids, prints, and textures. Think of your fabrics as dabs of color on an artist's palette. You will be using scissors and a sewing machine instead of a brush, scraps of fabric instead of paint. Just as an artist works on a blank canvas, you'll be sewing fabric, piece by piece, to a blank whole cloth foundation. Remember as you sew that successful foundation work depends on a mix of color, shapes, and textures.

ANTIQUE METHODS

Traditionalists may want to sew the whole project by hand, from running stitches to embroidery. Victorian women always hand-sewed the fabric pieces to a whole cloth foundation. Sometimes the foundation was the complete size of the finished quilt, but more often than not, the women worked on small blocks of foundation fabric that were later sewn together to form a whole quilt. In order to hide the angular block shapes, patches were sewn over the seams. The edges were turned under and blind-stitched in place. In some crazy quilts, the raw edges were not turned under and only tacked down with embroidery stitches. This proved unsatisfactory, as the fabric ravelled and did not stand up to regular use. Another method was to baste a large piece in place on the foundation and fit smaller pieces around it.

Victorian pattern books all preached the beauty of curved seams. They frowned on long, angular lines. Each and every seam was to be covered with fancy stitches. Above all, the sizes and shapes of fabric patches had to be asymmetrical.

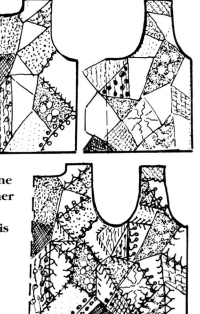

Hide That Seam!

To camouflage shoulder and side seams, leave the fabric on the outer edges hanging over the seam line. When it is time to sew the seam, peel back the loose edges on one side and trim the other edges even with the base. After the seam is sewn, appliqué the loose edges onto the adjacent piece, completely hiding the seam line.

TWO CONTEMPORARY METHODS

I delight in using the sewing machine for foundation work. I can finish in record time and get to the embellishing faster! My method involves string quilting with different shapes and sizes. Each piece is sewed onto its neighbor. Curved pieces are turned under to be appliquéd later. It is not necessary to press each fabric before it is sewn, but each piece must be pressed before the next piece is added.

Cut the foundation piece up to 2" (5 cm) larger than the desired finished size. On larger pieces, it is usually best to start in a corner and work outward in a fanlike progression. On smaller items, start with a center piece and work around it.

Once the base piece is completed, press it on both sides. Use spray starch or fabric sizing on the foundation back for extra stiffness. On pieces such as purses and pocket pouches, use iron-on interfacing. Trim all edges even with the foundation, unless you intend to join the foundation pieces and want to hide the seams.

"FAN" METHOD
Use this method for larger pieces.

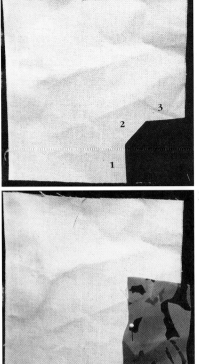

1. Cut a corner fabric patch with three or four angled sides Pin it in place flush with the bottom right corner of the foundation fabric.

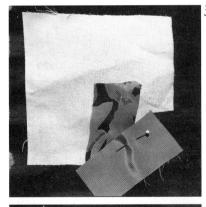

2. Select the next piece of fabric. Cut it into a wide rectangle. Lay it edge to edge on Angle 1, right sides together. Sew through the two pieces and the foundation fabric, from one end of Angle 1 to the other. Trim the seam. Flip the second piece over to its right side and press. If a tail of fabric hangs out, don't be concerned; it will be trimmed out after the next piece is sewn down.

3. Cut wide rectangles as you go. Be sure to alternate the colors as well as solids and patterns. Select the next fabric and lay it on Angle 2, making sure it extends over the previously sewn piece.

4. Sew from the outside edge of the previous piece to the edge of Angle 2. Trim away the excess fabric, then flip the piece to the right side and press.

5. Choose another rectangle. Cover Angle 3 and the piece just sewn down in the same manner. Trim out from behind, flip over, and press. Now you've completed the first clockwise level of the fan.

The next step is very important. You must cut angles from the rectangles just sewn down. Make sure you cut a variety of shapes and sizes. Then, starting at the bottom of the last piece sewn, begin working counterclockwise to lay down the next level.

6. Continue to fan back and forth, right to left, then left to right, until the foundation is completely filled. Always trim the excess fabric from the seams to keep the work from bulking up. Cut angles after each "wave," making sure you have a variety of shapes of sizes.

CENTER PIECE METHOD
Use this method for small items such as purses and jewelry.

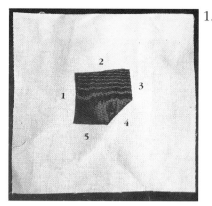

1. Cut a small piece with at least five angled sides from dark, solid fabric. (A dark fabric is preferable because it recedes and brings the eye to the center, making a good base for embroidery.) Pin the piece onto the foundation at the approximate center.

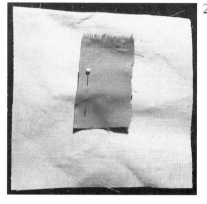

2. Cut a wide rectangle. Lay it along Angle 1, right sides together.

3. Sew from one edge of Angle 1 to the end. Flip the rectangle over to its right side, trim out from the seam, and press.

4. Cut a second wide rectangle and lay it against Angle 2. If you are right-handed, work clockwise, as shown. If you are left-handed, work counterclockwise. Be sure to cover the previous piece. Sew from the edge of the previous piece to the edge of the second angle. Cut out from behind and press flat.

5. Continue around until all the angles of the center piece are covered. Note than on Angle 5, the wide rectangle must extend over the pieces that cover both Angle 1 and Angle 4.

6. Now cut more angles from the pieces you have sewn down. Be sure to work towards a variety of shapes and sizes.

7. Continue adding pieces in a clockwise or counterclockwise direction. Keep a good balance of color, texture, patterns, and solids as you work. Remember to press as you go.

Rules to Remember

1. Always bounce color against color (blue against red, purple against teal, etc.).

2. Use a variety of solids, prints, and textures.

3. Never place print against print.

4. Always cover the previous piece of fabric.

5. Trim out from behind the seams.

6. Always press after the fabric piece has been sewn down.

7. Always use a wide rectangular piece of fabric. Cut the angles after sewing!

Fans. To fill an awkward V, follow the existing angle and add long, narrow triangles. The last side of the last triangle must be appliquéd by hand. Fans can also be presewn and added as a unit. They're great corner fillers.

Avoiding inside angles. If you try to use a small piece of fabric that does not fully cover the previous piece, you'll find yourself with a difficult inside angle. You can appliqué a small piece into the angle, or you can choose a piece of fabric with a longer edge and try again.

Curves.
Here's another solution to long edges. Press the seam allowance on the curved edge to the wrong side. Sew the straight edge of the piece in place, trace the curve onto the foundation, then flip the curved fabric back, out of the way of your sewing. Continue on with the crazy quilting, extending pieces just inside the traced curve. Appliqué the curved piece into place.

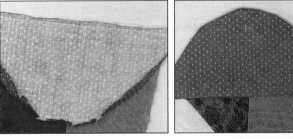

Prepieced strips. Long edges can be covered with strips pieced from assorted scraps. Be sure to use a variety of shapes and sizes. Use prepieced strips no more than necessary.

CRAZY QUILT LANDSCAPES

Crazy quilt landscapes are created much like oil paintings. The sky is laid in first, and the artist works down to the foreground. As you work, use darks to recede and lights to come forward. Try to mix burned edges with sewn angles and curves. Keep the shapes simple—you are creating the foundation for the textured embellishment that will follow.

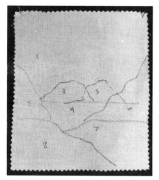

1. Make a rough sketch of the scene and number the pieces in the sequence they will be sewn in. Transfer this design to the base muslin.

2. Lay in the sky in first. Next come the distant mountains or hills. You can appliqué the edges or burn them (see page 71).

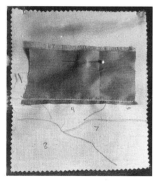

3. Once the furthest hills are in place, anchor them with a horizon line of fabric. Place right sides together, then fold over and press. Always place the horizon line off-center for a more pleasing effect.

4. Continue to work forward, adding features like rolling hills, water, and buildings, until you finish with the foreground.

Use window templates, cut from quilter's milky template plastic, to see exactly how a pattern piece will look when cut out from the crazy quilting. The milky plastic blocks out distracting details, yet lets you see shapes and color through it. Always cut the crazy quilt foundation larger than the pattern outline. This allows for shrinkage and gives you options for positioning the pattern. By moving the window around on the foundation, twisting and turning it for different views, you can choose just the right combination of color and shape. I use window templates in all my work, from large collars and bodices down to small pendants and earrings.

Hold down burned edges with tacky fabric glue until you can anchor them with embroidery or beading. Use a light hand—a toothpick or large darning needle is perfect to "dot" the glue onto the fabric.

Embellishments

Just how far can you take embellishments? A few years ago, Virginia Gray of McAllen, Texas, purchased *The Crazy Quilt Handbook* and was inspired to make the diamond center wall hanging. She sent me slides of her finished piece (Photo 39). Let me share some excerpts from her letter with you.

The outside black velvet border is . . . embellished with luxury cigarette premiums from the early 1900s. . . . [These] came in patriotic styles, or with pictures of pretty ladies, birds, butterflies, or . . . Oriental carpets such as those on my border. . . . The colorful antique floral ribbon, done entirely in a chain stitch, was a real find in an antique shop . . . and was just enough to finish off the diamond center and the inner [border] edge . . . . Antique shops and flea markets were a main source in searching for old buttons, jewelry, lace, and other old novelties which can be sewn or glued on. Beaded Victorian pieces such as the black one in the lower left corner are truly wonderful finds!

All of those little family heirlooms and memorabilia that you never knew how to use or what to do with—presto, you now have a solution! I used a bar pin (in diamond shape, upper right) made by my grandmother in 1887. She [made a macramé] lover's knot from her hair and in it placed her earrings and her husband's opal tie tack that they wore when they patch with a button from her wedding dress (1937), a locket with my father's picture, a locket from one of her childhood sweethearts, and pearl buttons from her mother's wedding dress (1910). . . . I added red star buttons in still another patch, reminiscing how, on clear moonlit nights, [we] would spread a quilt on the lawn and lying side by side, my little cousins, Grandmother, and I would face the heavens above and find the dippers and other constellations. I can remember her saying "I see the moon and the moon sees me!" Hence, the embroidered rendition of her little poem along with the man in the moon.

The "Virginia" patch came from a coat lining found in a vintage clothing store. With the name already beautifully executed, why not use it! There was a last name, but I appliquéd some little flowers over it, making my given name usable. I added my baby locket and booties, my birth date, and then 1988, the year of the quilt's completion.

[A] keepsake from great-grandfather is his black embroidered hat brought from the old country. The band is in the upper left and the top of the hat in the middle right. . . . For years, I've had a 1907 leather postcard floating aimlessly around from one drawer to another. . . . The little log cabin found a perfect dwelling place on the wall hanging. The card says "Home is the place we grumble the most but are treated the best", and under it in faded pen someone wrote "Ain't I right?"

[In] the upper right corner . . . embroidered fireworks explode above the exclamation "Liberty." A small aged American flag, . . . patriotic tobacco premiums, and a wonderful old White House button pay their respect [to] our American heritage. And to represent my own place in history, a button proudly lives on, plucked from oblivion where it once resided on my husband's long neglected Navy uniform. . . .

One very old piece of silk that I used was taken from an 1800s jacket. . . . Fortunately, an area around a pocket, embellished with a type of prairie point trim, was still strong enough to use. Looking at the old jacket made my thoughts go back to that day and time, wondering what special occasion it was made for, and envisioning its fashionable lady being carried by horse and buggy to some gala affair.

One could continue forever with this needle insanity. I just had to say, this is enough, I'm through with this one. My wall hanging now has its rightful place over the couch in my Victorian living room, which I decorated around my quilt, a piece of living family history.

When my students are struggling with the new technique of foundation work, I entice them on by saying "Just keep at it and this afternoon we'll get to the fun stuff!" Of course, I am referring to the embellishments. Everyone seems to agree that this is the best part of crazy quilting and the most creative. Even the most mundane and boring foundation can suddenly take on a magical appearance with layers of embellishments. Some students ask, "When is enough, enough?" I really don't know, as I have never reached that point! (Like Virginia Gray, I force myself to stop!)

Embellishments can be divided into "before" and "after." Those done before the foundation is sewn are the large decorations, such as embroidered pictures and photo transfers. These are worked onto large pieces of fabric that can be trimmed and shaped to fit into the foundation. The smaller embellishments are added in a set order, for ease of working and for saving time.

The choice of embellishments is personal. Do not feel you "must" add

<table>
<tr><td>"BEFORE"</td></tr>
<tr><td>Embroidered pictures</td></tr>
<tr><td>Paintings</td></tr>
<tr><td>Photo transfers</td></tr>
<tr><td>Punch needle</td></tr>
<tr><td></td></tr>
<tr><td>"AFTER"</td></tr>
<tr><td>Lace</td></tr>
<tr><td>Ribbons</td></tr>
<tr><td>Embroidery</td></tr>
<tr><td>Beads</td></tr>
<tr><td>Buttons</td></tr>
<tr><td>Doodads</td></tr>
<tr><td>Calligraphy</td></tr>
</table>

lots of lace, ribbons, and doodads. If you feel uncomfortable with frills and lace, them off and concentrate on spectacular embroidery and beading instead. No matter what embellishments you choose, working with them is never monotonous! In my travels, I keep coming across new items and techniques I can use in my crazy quilting, and I'm sure you will

too. In fact, many exciting ideas are passed on to me by my students!

VICTORIAN EMBROIDERY

COVERING SEAMS

The highlight of any Victorian crazy quilt is the intricate, endless variety of stitches that cover every seam. They make the crazy quilt foundation a thing of beauty, sparkling with pattern and color.

Don't be alarmed if your first stitches are uneven. Since design is created by repetition of line, just continue working the stitches unevenly until the seam is covered. If the stitches are too wide, keep them wide and persevere. On the next seam, you'll have the chance to make them more even and smaller. After a few hours, you will find you can

Detail: Dozens of embroidery stitch variations cover the seams of a Victorian era quilt.
PHOTO COURTESY DENVER ART MUSEUM

control the stitching better and it will become easier.

Start with the traditional stitches—such as herringbone stitch, cretan stitch, and feather stitch—that are illustrated in the Stitch Dictionary (page 124). Many traditional stitches are variations of each other. Combinations of traditional stitches—for example, buttonhole + French knot + lazy daisy—give a whole new look, especially if you use different colored threads.

Always choose threads several shades brighter than the foundation. They must be brighter in order to "sparkle." Bounce color off of color. Never put a blue thread against blue fabric; choose pink or gold instead. Embroidery takes a fair amount of time, and you will be disappointed if it does not show. To give your work added texture and dimension, try using silk and metallic threads, ribbon floss, silk ribbon, and variegated cottons. Short lengths (12" to 18", or 30 cm to 45 cm) should cover most seams.

CROSS-STITCH

Cross-stitch can be used in crazy quilting to commemorate names and dates or to record motifs from favorite pattern books. You can also highlight a painted background with cross-stitch. Choose a simple background and paint with fabric paints. Work the cross-stitch highlights with cotton floss and metallic threads. It's fast and easy—the perfect technique when you're looking for a quick gift idea.

Detail from the Kingwood friendship crazy quilt, given to the author by her guild friends in 1983.

RIBBON EMBROIDERY

While teaching in Australia, I was introduced to ribbon embroidery. It's a national pastime Down Under, and of course, I could hardly wait to try it in my crazy quilting. I've found it to be a marvelous form of embellishment. It's easy, fast, and very effective. You can use silk, velvet, satin, polyester, and rayon ribbons in various widths. With the ribbon, you work traditional embroidery stitches, usually ones that show most of the stitch on the right side. Some examples are the chain, cretan, and herringbone stitch.

Ribbon embroidery is an antique art that was very popular during the eighteenth and nineteenth centuries in Europe and Britain. The French royal court was especially fond of this decoration. Court dress for both men and women was elaborate and fancy, and beautiful garments were further embellished with ribbon by professional embroiderers.

Ribbon work appeared mostly in floral patterns along with silk floss and beads. Women wore it on fancy dresses and displayed it on accessories such as purses. Delicate, narrow silk ribbon was preferred, and most of the floral designs were worked in subtle shades. Ribbon work on men's clothing was perhaps more subtle. I have seen waistcoats decorated in sprays of flowers and collars and cuffs with beautiful white-on-white work.

> **Embroidery is like jewelry—it makes your work sparkle!**
> ♦ **Choose a large variety of colors.**
> ♦ **Use threads several shades brighter than the foundation.**
> ♦ **Bounce color off of color.**
> ♦ **Use a combination of thread types for textural and visual impact.**

Detail of a jewelry box lid featuring ribbon embroidery and antique laces. Silk ribbon embroidery by Gloria McKinnon, Newcastle, New South Wales, Australia.

MATERIALS AND SUPPLIES

The supplies for ribbon embroidery are easily obtained.

❧ **Needles.** You will need a variety of needles with eyes big enough to accommodate the ribbon. Purchase tapestry, crewel, and chenille needles in assorted sizes.

❧ **Ribbon.** Be sure to have a good range of colors—remember, you are creating flowers that are shaded, not all one color. Kanagawa silk ribbons provide a choice of over one hundred colors. I prefer silk ribbons because they are lovely, pliable, and washable. The narrow 2 mm and 4 mm widths are dainty, traditional, and easy to use. Polyester ribbons have more spring and are sometimes difficult to pull through the fabric. In this case, a sewing stiletto comes in handy for poking holes in the fabric, making it easier to finish the stitch.

❧ **Embroidery Thread.** Again, you will need a variety of colors. Floss is available in silk and cotton. I use yards of silk buttonhole twist. It gives a lovely sheen to the work, and through Kanagawa I work with a palette of over two hundred colors! Pearl cotton in sizes 8 and 5 is thicker than floss and is good for anchor stitches, leaves, and stems. Matching sewing thread is used to tack down roses and ribbons. Metallic and other novelty threads can be useful too. Use your imagination!

❧ **Scissors.** Keep sharp embroidery scissors and regular sewing scissors on hand..

❧ **Embroidery Hoop.** Traditionally, a hoop is used for ribbon embroidery, though I find small pieces of crazy quilting are easier to work held in the hand. The beauty of ribbon embroidery is its three-dimensional effect. Hoops tend to smash the stitches, so be especially careful when you change the hoop position.

❧ **Fabric.** A firm, tightly woven fabric is best. Cotton velveteen, silk, linen, cotton, wool, rayon, and many polyester blends are fine as long as they are firm. Beginners should avoid knit fabrics, leather, and sheers. I have worked with Ultrasuede and knits, but they are more difficult to manage. Ultrasuede needs to be punched every stitch with a stiletto, and knits are wiggly and stretchy.

GETTING STARTED

Professional ribbon embroiderers leave about ¼" (6 mm) of ribbon on the wrong side of the work when they start. After part of the work is complete, they go back and sew down the ends with cotton thread. They finish the same way. I'm not so particular—I just put a knot in the end and carry on! ! Most of the time I'm using narrow silk ribbon so the knot is not bulky, but I do concede to the proper method when using wide ribbons.

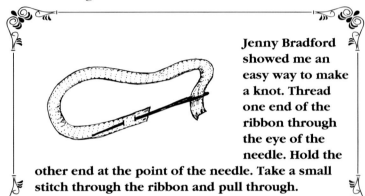

Jenny Bradford showed me an easy way to make a knot. Thread one end of the ribbon through the eye of the needle. Hold the other end at the point of the needle. Take a small stitch through the ribbon and pull through.

MARKING THE DESIGN

The design is marked on the right side of the fabric, but unlike other embroidery, where every line must be marked, ribbon embroidery uses a simple series of dots. For small items, such as necklaces, needlecases, and earrings, you need only mark the largest flower with a dot (use a pencil or water-soluble pen). You work the rest of the design by referring to the pattern. On larger pieces, such as garments, pillows, and wall hangings, try to have a more specific design.

A light box is excellent for transferring the design. You can also simply tape the fabric and pattern to a window and trace. In Australia, the women transfer the design to netting and then place the net over the fabric. Dots and simple lines are transferred with white pencil (on dark fabrics), pen, or water-soluble pens. The netting is removed before stitching.

CREATING DIMENSION

Ribbon, of course, is not a thread but a flat width. Therefore, your thumb takes on a new importance! To keep the ribbon flat when stitching, hold it in place with your thumb. Many of the designs or flowers look better with a twist—use your own judgment. Learn to think dimensionally. In other words, what flowers are out front? Which flower is the largest? What flowers are peeking out from behind? Above all, learn to work loosely. The stitches are much more effective and will look more natural. For effective design and scale, make the stitches in proportion to the size of the ribbon.

For more creative designs, mix threads and ribbons. Try using thread for vines, leaves, and tiny knot flowers, pearl cotton for anchor stitches, and silk buttonhole twist for leaves and stems.

STITCH GUIDE

Here's how some stitches look and are worked in ribbon embroidery. For a closer look at basic stitch steps, see the Stitch Dictionary.

Cretan Stitch. Start in the lower left corner and work from left to right. Make short vertical stitches alternately downward and upward. Hold the ribbon with the thumb and let the needle pass over it. Stitches can be spaced close together or apart. Very good for textures.

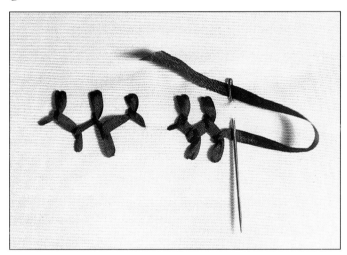

Cross-Stitch. A simple stitch that looks effective as a cross or an X. The stitch lengths can be varied for a different effect. A small catch stitch at the intersection creates yet another variation.

Featherstitch (also known as the briar stitch or turkey tracks). A vertical stitch that is worked down towards you. The secret is to always put the needle in at B, straight across from where the thread came out at A. It can be worked singly (fly stitch), in

groups with long and short tails, or in a chain to give a feather effect.

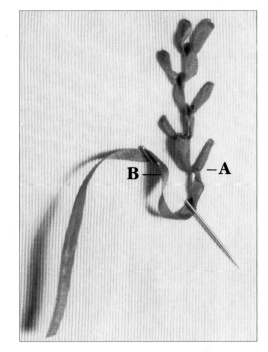

Herringbone Stitch. Work from left to right, making sure that the ribbon lies evenly on both sides of the seam. Take a small, horizontal back stitch on each side, equidistant from the seam line. Use your thumb to keep the ribbon flat.

Lazy Daisy. Think of this loop stitch as a free-floating chain stitch. Bring the ribbon up from the back and hold it down with your thumb. Insert the needle again at the starting point. Bring it out a short distance away, making sure the needle comes up over the ribbon. Take a small holding stitch at the top of the loop.

Spiderweb Roses. With pearl cotton, work a fly stitch, then add a straight stitch to each side of the fly stitch into the center point. Bring the ribbon through the center point and weave over and under the spokes until the web is filled. Weave loosely and allow occasional twists.

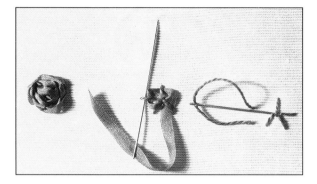

Twisted Chain Stitch. This stitch makes a beautiful flower bud. Bring the ribbon up and form a loop by crossing over the ribbon and inserting the needle slightly to the left. Finish off at the bottom with small catch stitch.

Whipped Chain Stitch. Work a continuous chain stitch with embroidery floss. Whip over each stitch with a matching or contrasting ribbon.

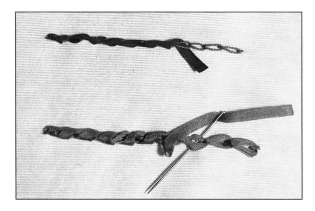

The Jenny Bradford Rose

Jenny Bradford is a lovely Australian who is a ribbon embroidery expert. She has written three books on the subject and her work is exquisite. Here is a rose of her own design that is firm and wears well. The rose is quick and easy and can be worked in any width of ribbon in one to three shades.

Beginning with the darkest shade, work a single loose French knot for the center. Work three whipped stitches in a clockwise direction around the center knot. Anchor each stitch with a central catch for a slight curve. Work four or five whipped stitches around the previous round, anchoring each in a slight curve.

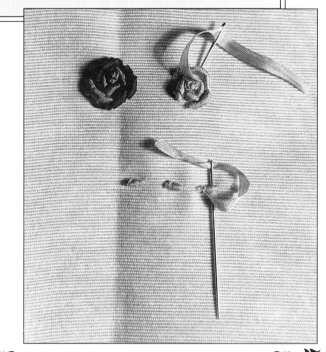

Finishing Hints

♦ Once your stitching is complete, gently press with a steam iron from the back. Lay the piece face down into a thick terry towel. Do not flatten the work.

♦ For a stiffer, more professional look, use iron-on interfacing. I always add interfacing right after the base work is done. Any embroidery, beading, and embellishment threads are carried right through it to the back!

♦ Pad box lid inserts and pictures with Pellon® Fleece. It gives a softer, more rounded look to the mounted piece.

DESIGN WORK

Ribbon embroidery can enhance your quilting, ready-to-wear garments, and other needlework. Like quilting, it needs to be carefully thought out, especially in clothing or any item requiring seams.

- ◆ **Keep the design in proportion** to the piece you are working. If the piece is small, make the design delicate. If it is large, scale the pattern into a bolder and larger design.
- ◆ **Display your work.** On clothing, always work the embroidery where it will enhance the overall design. Make sure it integrates into the garment and doesn't stick out like a sore thumb.
- ◆ **Work over seams.** Ribbon embroidery can meander over many seams for a collage effect. Trace a replica of the assembled pattern pieces and carefully mark the seam lines. If your design is going to flow over a seam line, sew the seam beforehand, press it open, and then carry on with the embroidery.
- ◆ **Embellish!** I like to highlight ribbon work with beads and metallic threads. Don't be afraid to use a large variety of threads. In small pendants, the center piece can be decorated with ribbon embroidery and further collaged with doodads and beads. Pearl buttons can be added to ribbon bouquets as embellished flowers. Let your imagination take hold and don't hesitate in mixing different techniques.

PUNCH NEEDLE EMBROIDERY

Years ago I met punch needle expert Jean Cook, who is responsible for the interest on the West

Coast. I've learned most of what I know about this exciting needle art from her and Marinda Stewart.

Punch needle embroidery is a Russian technique in which looped stitches are punched from the back of the fabric to the front. The embroidery is done with a tiny handcrafted needle threaded with one to six strands of embroidery floss. The fabric is tightly stretched across an embroidery hoop, and the design is worked with the needle on the wrong side. This results in tiny loops that create a thick, plush raised design on the right side. No knotting is done. The finished

Victorian teddy bears are very popular in Australia. This fellow, made by Pam Hicks of Newcastle, New South Wales, is sewn from fancy pastel fabrics and Liberty of London cottons. Each seam is carefully embroidered with silk ribbon flowers and beads.

work is durable and washable.

The history of the craft is obscure, but it is believed to have originated centuries ago in the Ukraine. The original needle was made from a thin sheet of tin, finely rolled and secured with tightly coiled wire or thread. The art of punch needle embroidery was brought to Europe, America, and Canada by a group called the Russian Old Believers. They became known as Old Believers as early as 1660, when they refused to accept the reform of the rites of the Russian Orthodox Church and were excommunicated. For hundreds of years they fled persecution, migrating to Siberia, China, Brazil, the United States, and Canada. Old Believers in these communities have deliberately isolated themselves from other cultural influences and marry only within the group in order to keep their own culture and religion intact. The men do not shave, nor do the women cut their hair.

Traditional Russian punch needle was used to embellish men's shirts, women's blouses, curtains,

Detail from the jacket of "Exotic Gypsy Escapade" showing punch needle embroidery in DMC® floss and silk ribbon.

stitches show up on the spot, not rows later as they can in counted work. I often use punch needle in crazy quilting because it mixes very well with silk painting and ribbon embroidery. Punch needle can be considered a method of painting with threads. The smaller the needle, the finer the detail.

MATERIALS AND SUPPLIES

Punch needle is a relatively inexpensive hobby. You'll need needles, tightly woven fabric, hoop, floss, and embroidery scissors.

✿ **Punch Needles.** The punch needle itself is usually a small, hollow shaft with a metal handle. It is threaded through the shaft and up through the eye of the needle. There are many types of punch needles on the market today, and each and every one works on the same principle.

✿ **Fabrics.** Always use a tightly woven fabric. Suitable fabrics for this work are medium to heavy weight and include chambray, muslin, cotton, cotton/polyester, silk, most wash-and-wear fabrics, cotton velveteen, taffeta, corduroy, and heavy denim. I use cotton, silk, moiré, and cotton velveteen for crazy quilting. Beginners should start out with a basic cotton weave and save the cotton velveteen and silks till later. Ultrasuede and extremely delicate or stretchy fabrics can be used but require special handling.

Like ribbon embroidery, punch needle embroidery can be worked on clothing and accessories.

icon panels, and wall hangings. Brilliantly colored floral designs are the most common motifs. Westerners' applications of the craft includes miniature Oriental doll rugs, textile jewelry, decorated clothing, and soft sculpture. The back of the work is considered by some to be as exquisite as the front, and many are experimenting by combining the right and "wrong" sides in their designs. The depth of the pile can be changed and the pile can also be clipped or sheared to give a velvetlike texture.

Throughout the world, there are many adaptations of the punch needle. The Japanese bunka needle is used to punch crinkly rayon threads at different stitch lengths to form lovely pictures and wall hangings. The looped side is the back of bunka! In India, a rough, primitive needle made of rolled tin is used to create beautiful punch needle designs in brightly colored wool and cotton.

The beauty of punch needle embroidery for the crafter is its speed and effectiveness. It looks much more difficult than it is. Very little can go wrong, but when it does, you will know immediately! Messy or skipped

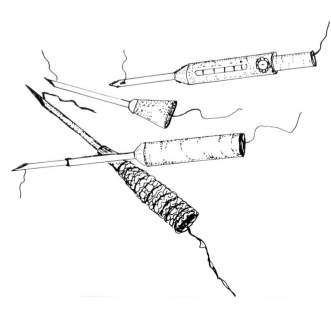

Plan and complete the needlework before construction, and leave ample seam allowances for mistakes. I prefer to draw the cutting edge onto the fabric and then cut 2" (5 cm) beyond that.

✿ **Embroidery Hoop.** The fabric must be held drum-tight in an embroidery hoop. The traditional method is to wrap the inner ring of a wooden embroidery hoop with yarn. Also on the market are machine embroidery hoops and several good plastic hoops that have a holding "lip."

➤ **Threads.** Traditionally, cotton floss is used, but today's assorted needle sizes can accommodate silk threads, metallics, yarns, and even silk ribbon!

GETTING STARTED

Designs can be taken from basic embroidery books, children's coloring books, and crewel patterns. If the fabric is a light color, use a light box for tracing onto the back of the fabric. If you cannot see the design, try using a transfer pencil. Trace the design onto tracing paper, then iron the transfer onto the fabric. Remember that since the design is punched from the back, it will face the opposite way on the front. Make sure the design is facing the proper direction!

USING THE PUNCH NEEDLE

1. Start out with a simple design and a medium size needle that will take about three strands of floss. Make sure the fabric is drum tight in the embroidery hoop or the stitches will not hold.
2. Closely examine your needle. On the pointed end, one side is open and cut at an angle. On the other side is a small eye.

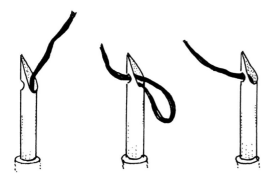

3. The open side must always be facing in the direction in which you are stitching. The thread must be coming up at the top through the eye.
4. Hold the needle much like a pencil. Relax your hand and do not hold too tight. Make sure the thread coming out the end of the handle is not obstructed.
5. Insert the needle into the fabric and push it all the way down until the stitch gauge stops it. Hold the needle at about a 70 ° angle. I like to use the angle of the cut side of the needle as a guide.
6. Lift the needle back to the surface and drag it along to the next stitch—about ⅟₃₂" (1 mm)—and repeat. Think of it as punch, drag, punch, drag! Do not lift the needle off of the surface. Doing so will cause messy and skipped loops.

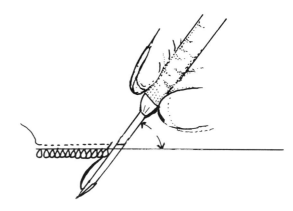

7. Once the thread is used up, cut it off flush at the back.
8. If you need to remove stitches, simply pull them out. Be sure to realign the fabric threads by scratching over the surface. Do not reuse the thread. Cut this portion off.
9. Outline the design in a darker shade to highlight it, then fill in with various colors and shades. Simply lay rows of punch needle embroidery down side by side. For best, results the rows should follow the contour of the shape being filled.
10. Like any other technique, punch needle embroidery requires practice, but it does not take long to get the stitches small and even. On my new desert scenes, I am able to complete the piece right up to the embroidery and then punch in the grass and tree leaves through more than one layer. Adjust the gauges on the punch needle for loops of various depths.

SPECIAL TECHNIQUES

Shearing. Set the punch needle gauge at a long loop. Fill in the design with close, even stitches. Using sharp embroidery scissors, cut the loops shorter and to one length. This gives a velour texture. Also notice that once the threads are sheared, the color becomes more intense by at least one shade—a great bonus, because you get two color variations with one thread.

Sculpting. This technique is like shearing, only the piece is taken out of the hoop for trimming. The goal is to create a rounded mound. After filling in

with long loops, take the fabric in one hand and roll the area to be sculpted over your index finger. This gives better control because the edges of the sculpted design must be shorter than the center. Clip the edges first with sharp embroidery scissors. Keep the piece rolled on your finger. Angle the scissors toward the center and clip up towards the center. The flowers that use this technique include pussy willows, wattle, and thistle.

Feathering. The design area is punched and sheared. Keeping the same long loop, go back over the sheared area with a finer thread, such as silk or metallic. Randomly punch in long, wispy loops. This makes a beautiful effect for the center of flowers, to highlight bird feathers, or to add texture to landscape pictures.

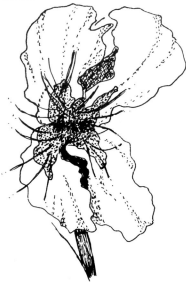

Metallic Work. There are so many beautiful metallic threads on the market today. Unfortunately, they come in a wide variety of qualities and sizes, which can be confusing for the beginner.

Filament metallic threads are delicate and wispy and good for feathering. The metallic is spun loosely around a core thread. For more glitter, pair the thread with a single strand of embroidery floss and treat the two strands as one. The glitter will show even more if the threads are in the same color family.

Machine embroidery metallics are much stronger than filament threads, and I recommend them for

embroidery as well as punch needle. They have a very smooth, spun feel and will stand up to heavier use. Because they are rather wiry, use them in a single strand needle and punch with a short gauge. They can also be blended with other threads.

Metallic mixes include cotton and woolly threads that have metallics blended in. These are made especially for the punch needle craft industry. They are thicker and will require a larger needle.

Flat metallics will crinkle when they are twisted. These are better left for couching or embroidery. Try using them in a six-strand needle, but be aware of the pitfalls.

Ribbon Punch Needle. Narrow silk and polyester ribbons make the most effective punch needle flowers—a marvelous design technique for clothing. Try ⅛", ¼", 2 mm, or 4 mm ribbon widths, and make sure the punch needle is big enough to let the ribbon flow freely. Polyester ribbon should be the bias type sold for knitting and crochet, not the flat satin-polyester type. It will have more "bounce" than silk.

Reverse Work. The back of punch needle embroidery looks like a series of small, running stitches and can be very effective. Use it on the front of the design for stems, tendrils, tree branches, landscape texture, and even writing. I sign many of my pieces this way. This method is also used in candlewicking and needlepoint punch.

Landscape Texturing. Set the needle at a longer loop to punch through more than one layer. For best results, baste the layers together. This way your loops will not wedge or get lost between the layers. In landscape crazy quilting, the punch needle is done after the Victorian stitches have been applied.

The punch needle technique: The fabric is secured drum-tight in a hoop and the design is punched from the back. The needle is held like a pencil, so that the thread comes up over the hand.

FINE LINE SKETCHING AND CALLIGRAPHY

You can draw or write on your crazy quilt with permanent pens. They come in a variety of sizes and colors, including metallics. Use them for outline tracing, cross-hatching, and retracing over fabrics that have been painted. Poetry, quotations, and signatures always add a personal effect. Use your best penmanship or hire someone who specializes in calligraphy. Quotations from family diaries and autographed fabric photos will deepen the value of a family crazy quilt. Be sure to test the pen on a scrap of fabric first.

PAINTING ON FABRIC

If you have ever drawn or painted on paper, you will love working on fabric. It opens up a whole new world. Perhaps you'll want to immortalize a childhood memory, a home, or a special area of the country. But don't stop there! Punch needle, ribbon, and free-form embroidery all take on a deeper dimension when worked over a painted background.

There are many fabric paints on the market. Most come in squeeze bottles in a wide variety of colors. The paint can be used right out of the bottle for a painterly look, or it can be watered down and used like watercolors. Paints can mixed for shading. I like acrylics because they dry quickly and I can come in right away with permanent pens and needlework. Acrylics dry quickly on the brush too, so be sure to rinse well!

Start out with simple designs. These can be achieved with sponges or large brushes. Turn to nature for shapes and inspiration. Leaves make wonderful printing tools. Simply paint the veined side of the leaf and lay it down on the fabric. Lift up and lay down again.

Be sure to wear old clothes and an apron when working with pigments or dyes. Cover your work area with plastic. All fabric paints need to be set with an iron. To ensure permanence on pieces to be worn, use a pressing cloth soaked in vinegar. Protect your iron from still-wet paints with a clean pressing cloth.

The author's favorite saying is forever emblazoned on a wall hanging. A permanent Pilot® SC-UF pen was used.

A chicken family painted with Setacolor® fabric paint hovers over a punch needle egg. Detail of a pillow created by Alice Bertling, a well-known regional artist from Kingwood, Texas, whose sense of humor always shows in her work.

PIGMENT PAINTS

Yvonne Porcella is an expert in the fabric painting field and has given me some special hints for using fabric pigment paints. Pigment paints are also known as silk paints, but they can be used on almost any fabric. Natural fibers work best. For best results, stick to 100% cotton or silk. Yvonne prefers silk because it tears easily for her strip piecing. She uses silk pongee, silk voile, china silk, and silk twill.

Limit your colors to begin with and experiment with color mixing (refer to the color wheel). Red, yellow, and blue will give you the basics. Yvonne suggests adding green and magenta to this palette. Be careful not to use excessive pigment as it will build up on the surface and make the fabric stiff. To achieve dark, intense colors, Yvonne uses fiber-reactive dyes instead.

Yvonne Porcella's *A Colorful Book* features six different techniques for fabric dyeing and painting. Once a year I buy "sky fabric" from Yvonne to use in my pictorial crazy quilting. I am a slob with dyes and pigments. Everything from the walls to my toes get colored, so I go to the expert for my sky fabric! See the Source Guide for her address.

> ### Yvonne's Butcher Paper Method
> Here is a fun method of fabric painting that will give you two results—beautiful fabric AND wrapping paper!
>
> You will need:
> ➻ White butcher paper
> ➻ Pigment paints (thinned with water)
> ➻ Silk fabric (white)
> ➻ Plastic covering
>
> 1. Crush and scrunch the butcher paper. Lay it out on the plastic covering. Be sure the paper has lots of "hills and valleys."
> 2. Dampen the fabric and lay it down onto the butcher paper. Thin the pigment with water.
> 3. Pour on the pigment paints and wait. The raised areas will become lighter and the valley areas darker.
> 4. Let both the fabric and the paper dry.
> 5. Iron the fabric.
> 6. Iron the butcher paper too, and voilà, you have dyed wrapping paper . . . à la Yvonne Porcella!

Box lid created by the author to depict a scene along the Zane Gray Trail in New Mexico. Sky fabric was hand-dyed by Yvonne Porcella. Hills are Thai silk. Note the punch needle shrubbery and ant and spider earrings.

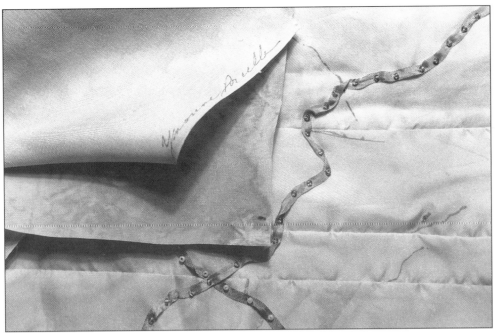

Detail of a striped vest overlaid with Yvonne Porcella dyed silk and a meandering twisted ribbon.

TRANSFER PAINTS AND CRAYONS

Does the thought of painting directly onto fabric scare you? Do you want a surer method? Try using transfer paints and crayons. The design can be traced onto paper and then colored in. There are two points to remember:

♦ Just like an embroidery transfer, the image is reversed.

♦ Colors will vary according to the fabric type.

Transfer paints and crayons are made for use on synthetics and will color them intensely. On cottons and silks, the color is very subtle. A single design can be ironed on several times, but each application will be more faded. If you can, come in later with pigment paints or acrylics and finish off with embroidery highlights.

For inspiration and ideas, I recommend *The Art of Embroidery* by Julia Barton. She combines painting, sketching, and free-form embroidery like no one else. Her book has become one of my favorites.

FABRIC DYES

Dyes can be used in the same way as fabric paints. The beauty of dye is that it does not build on the surface but is absorbed into the fabric. You will notice that dyed fabric is much softer and more pliable than painted fabric and that it is the same intensity on both sides.

Since dyes are permanent, I suggest working with a good teacher or shop that has the proper facilities. There are several types of dyes—steam-fixed, liquid-fixed, and iron-fixed. There are many good products on the market today (see Source Guide).

Detail of "Nancy Halpern's Maine." Silk fabrics painted by Yvonne Porcella and Roslyn Morton appear together for the background. Transfer paints bring shadows to the water.

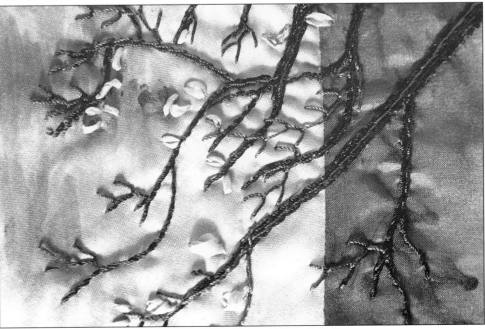

A cat contemplates his day while nesting on his favorite pillow. Painted by artist Alice Bertling with Setacolor fabric paints.

MARBLEIZING

Marbleizing is a method of floating paints on top of a water-carrageen solution. By "raking" the paints with a wide comb, you can make various patterns. The fabric is gently laid down on the solution and the paint adheres to it. I give an easy marbleizing recipe that uses acrylic paint, water, and carrageen in *The Crazy Quilt Handbook.*

You can use marbleizing to "paint" paper, Ultrasuede, and leather. Or create your own special silk fabric to pull together an outfit. Try it— you'll love it!

PHOTOGRAPHY ON FABRIC

Thanks to current technologies, we can now transfer images to cloth with ease. Businesses that print images on T-shirts can be found almost everywhere; some will reduce the size for you onto yardage. The photocopier lets us reproduce favorite photos and memorabilia without the expense of negatives. Here are some ideas you can try at home with a little technical help from the pros in your community.

AUSTRALIAN PHOTOCOPYING

In Australia, I met a lovely lady—Janet Power of Ultima, Victoria—and she gave me a recipe for transposing photographs to fabric that is quick and easy. Her quilt group used this method on its bicentennial quilt.

You'll need:
- ➥ Clear photograph, magazine picture, or card
- ➥ Turpentine
- ➥ Ink blotting paper
- ➥ Large spoon
- ➥ Cosmetic puffs
- ➥ Silk organza or cotton batiste*

*The fabric must be a natural fiber, very thin and quite sheer. The image will not adhere to polyester fabrics.

1. Make a photocopy of the photograph or card. Make sure it is crisp and clear. (Colored inks such as sepia tone work well.)
2. Lay the fabric on top of the blotting paper.
3. Lay the photocopy face down onto the fabric.
4. Soak the cotton ball in the turpentine and rub on the back of the photocopy. You will see the paper become translucent, as if oil had been spilled on it. Soak the area well, but don't get it soppy.

Three photo transfer techniques: The antique postcard was heat-transferred with a copy machine; hankie was printed by the Australian turpentine method; boy is a sun print on muslin.

5. Rub the back of the spoon firmly across the photocopy. Rub evenly, holding the photocopy down with the other hand. When you are satisfied that you've covered the whole area, lift up.

6. Note that the image is reversed. If you've used sheer organza, just turn it over so the image faces correctly (especially good with text!).

I have really enjoyed this method. It saves my lovely old photographs and the cost of having negatives made. I've taken images from cards, postcards, books, and magazines. I'm currently working on a special quilt documenting the women in my family. I'm using their photographs and handkerchiefs to make a crazy quilt collage.

CYANOTYPE PRINTING

Cyanotype printing is also referred to as sun printing or blueprint photography. It is one of the simplest photographic processes—you can do it in your own backyard on a sunny day. You'll need special chemically treated fabric, a photo negative, and a piece of glass. The chemicals and directions for using them are available from a number of reputable manufacturers through craft shops and by mail-order (see Source Guide). Some companies offer pretreated fabrics so you don't have to mix the chemicals yourself.

The possibilities these fabric photographs provide are endless! You can record the family's history, commemorate weddings, births, and anniversaries, tell a story, or document local history.

HOW TO GET SEPIA TONES

Sometimes you may not want the brilliant blue of the cyanotype. Here is a recipe to give your fabric prints a sepia (brown) antiqued look.

1. **To pull out the blue color, use:**
   - **1 tablespoon of phosphate detergent (powdered Tide)**
   - **2 cups tap water**

   Stir the detergent into the water, making sure it is well dissolved.

2. **Place the printed fabric into the solution until it turns pale yellow.**

3. **Rinse the fabric in clear water.**

4. **Prepare a tea solution with:**
   - **2 cups boiling water**
   - **3 tea bags (use orange pekoe or pekoe black tea)**

   Pour the water over the tea bags and steep for 5 minutes.

5. **Pour the tea into a flat PYREX® dish. Lay the printed fabric face down into the tea solution and soak for 30 minutes.**

6. **Rinse in cold water and line-dry.**

HOW IT WORKS

The word *cyanotype* is derived from the Greek words meaning "dark blue image." The blue is caused from the reaction of exposed iron salt chemicals to ultraviolet rays. The photo negative (or other flat object, such as a leaf) is placed on the treated fabric and "exposed" to the sun. The blue forms the shadows and the blocked areas remain white. Once the fabric is rinsed with water, the image becomes permanent.

Sun printing requires the use of a sharp negative. On high contrast prints, continuous tone film negatives can be used. For antique photographs, or photos that are mostly gray tones, your best image may be a black and white litho negative. Often the companies that sell sun printing supplies specialize in making negatives from old prints. You can also check with lithographers to make photo positives on acetate. Ask them to group several photographs together for economy.

USING THE PHOTOCOPIER

Cyanotype prints can also be produced with the help of the photocopier. Set the machine at its darkest and use acetate film in place of paper. Make two copies and tape them together to make a sharper image. Remember that the film will be a positive image and the resulting print will be a negative—perhaps not so good for photographs and text, but a lot of fun with flat objects, silhouettes, and drawings. Cover the acetate "print" with glass during exposure to make a good contact print. Leaves, flowers, and grass may be laid directly onto the treated fabric. Other objects such as lace, tools, and paper cutouts will make beautiful designs. Let your imagination run wild!

COLOR PHOTOCOPIES

Color photocopying opens yet another new door for crazy quilting. Now we can imitate the lovely antique cigarette silks and advertising ribbons!

Phone around your area until you find a printer who has a laser color copier. Ask for heat transfer paper. It is used in the heat transferring of images onto garments and patches and  adheres well to 100% cotton, 50%/50% blends, and 100% polyester. Birthday and wedding cards, postcards, photographs, invitations, magazine pictures, and similar items can be transferred onto the heat transfer paper by photocopier. If there is printing on the piece, you must make a copy onto a transparency and then make a reverse copy from that. Feed the heat transfer paper into the copy machine glossy side down. Cut away the unprinted area.

Applying the transfer to the fabric requires heat. You can take the transfer to a sweatshirt shop and have it done on a press pad. It should be pressed at 375°F for 20 seconds with maximum pressure. Remove it while hot. To do the transfer yourself at home, preheat the iron for 10 minutes on a low cotton setting. Do not use steam. Slide a piece of cardboard under the fabric, then place the transfer, color side down, on the fabric. Press every inch of the transfer for 20 seconds each. Lean into the iron with both hands and use body pressure for best results. Immediately reheat the entire area by making three complete circles with the iron. Begin in one corner and peel the transfer from the fabric while hot.

This printed fabric can be washed in cool or warm water only. Do not use bleach or iron over the transfer. You've learned another way of transferring memories to fabric, only this time it is in color!

BEADS

Beads are a passion of mine, and I use them as much as possible. They can accent Victorian stitches, ribbon embroidery, and punch needle. I often use them in place of French knots or to

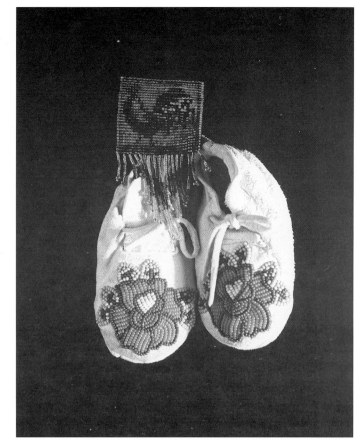

Three styles of beadwork: Beads on the moccasin are laid down in rows and couched; made by Mrs. Lefthand of the Stoney Indian Reserve, Morley, Alberta, Canada. Featherstitching is highlighted by single beads at the end of each stitch. The rooster brooch was a gift to the author by Japanese loom beading expert Tokuko Udagawa.

highlight a patterned fabric. Beads add shimmer, sheen, and that final sparkle!

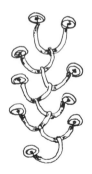

MATERIALS AND SUPPLIES

🍂 **Beads.** Good beads come in a wide variety of shapes, sizes, colors, and finish. They range from miniscule to large pony and trade beads (see Findings). For crazy quilting, keep beads in the #10 to #13 range. I use an average size #11 bead.

≈ **Needles.** Beading needles come in two types, sharps and shorter. A good rule of thumb is to use a needle size about one number higher than the bead size. Even so, I use a #10 sharps to sew on individual #11 beads and have little trouble with the beads sliding through.

Bead Size	Needle Size
10	11
11	12
11 or 12	13
12 or 13	14

A long, thin needle, simply called a beading needle, is used to pick up long rows of beads for couching down. All needles eventually get metal fatigue and the eye slots get thinner from use. Realize your eyes aren't playing tricks on you and keep replacing your beading needles! (This hint is from expert Jeanne Leffingwell.)

≈ **Thread.** Take care to use beading thread. Many people use silk or cotton thread, but after years of wear and tear, it will break down. Nylon craft line may look good, but it stretches and melts under the iron. I recommend Nymo ® thread by Belding Corticelli for beadwork. It is made just for beading and comes in various weights. It looks like dental floss and is available at most craft shops (see Source Guide).

GETTING STARTED

Pour the beads out into a large shallow white plate. You need to be able to see the beads as well as let your hand rest in the plate without tipping it. Plastic convenience dinner plates work well.

Examine a bead and you'll see how the shine and color are on its side, not on the hole ends. To show on your crazy quilting, the bead must be pulled taut to sit up on its side. The Nymo thread has a bit of give to it, and after the first pull, it holds the beads in position.

Beads used to highlight embroidery are sewn on one at a time with a #10 sharps needle. Bring the needle up at the point of the stitch, pick up a bead on the needle, then go back down a few fabric threads from the initial hole. Pull the thread with a bounce (the thread will twang) to secure the bead up on

its side. Go on to the next stitch and do the same. To hold the beads and ensure that only a few will be lost if the thread breaks, tie a knot at the back of every fifth bead. You can use beads to highlight featherstitch, cretan stitch, herringbone stitch, buttonhole stitch, and others.

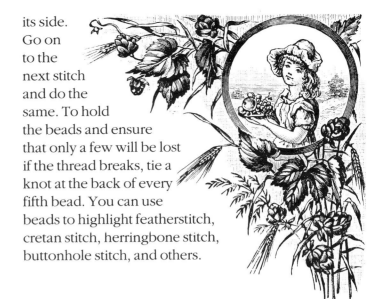

AVOIDING FATIGUE

Beading expert Jeanne Leffingwell reminds us that a good worker always takes care of her tools. Your body is your most valuable instrument, so treat it well.

- ❧ Work under good light.
- ❧ Take frequent breaks to rest your eyes.
- ❧ Try working at a high table so that your elbows are at chest level when seated. (I suffered for years from neck and shoulder problems. By raising my table eight inches, my aches and pains disappeared.)
- ❧ Get rid of bad beads immediately when you pick them up on the needle to avoid further frustration. Those too small holes and rough edges have a way of reappearing time and again!

SPECIAL TECHNIQUES

Couched Beadwork. It is easier to lay down lines of beads when you use the long, thin beading needle. Hold the needle at a low angle and use the index finger to pick up the beads from the plate. Lay the line of beads down onto the fabric in the desired postion. Insert the needle down through the fabric, then come up and down, couching down every bead. Use this one-thread method to couch short lines of beads.

For longer lines, use the two-thread method. Gather up a long line of beads and hold the thread in place with a pin. Come up with a separate thread and couch each bead into place.

When American Indian women first obtained beads for their embroidery, they sewed them to buckskin in two ways:

Spot Stitch. Spot stitch is known to us as couching. A thread of sinew strung with a line of beads was attached to the buckskin by another sinew thread sewed across it.The bead thread was pulled up through the leather and positioned on top, and the sewing thread pierced the top layer of the leather between beads.

Later, the Plains Indians started couching every three or four beads and called it the Lazy Stitch.

Lazy Squaw Method. The western Sioux used geometric designs that did not require couching. They worked out a method where a number of beads (from six to twelve) were strung on the sinew. The sinew was inserted into a hole poked by an awl and up through another hole. Then another group of beads was strung, and the process was repeated.

Loom Beading. Early loom beading was done by the Indian women on a bow strung with a number of wrap strings. It was widely adapted by the Sioux in their geometric designs. Today there are many types of looms and books on the subject. The beads can be arranged according to a chart and amazing designs can be made. Finished projects can be sewn down to crazy quilting.

> My friend Tokuko Udagawa from Tokyo, Japan, is an expert at loom beading. Several months ago, I wrote to her on my letterhead, which features three chickens. On my next visit to Japan, she presented me with a beautiful evening bag adorned with my three chickens and a rooster brooch. Her husband had charted the design from my letterhead, and Tokuko made it on a bead loom!

BUTTONS AND DOODADS

BUTTONS

Buttons add texture and dimension as well as a touch of nostalgia to crazy quilting. Save them for the final application as they add bulk and weight to the piece. You'll find buttons in antique shops, garage sales, and secondhand shops, as well as fabric shops. Pearl buttons have a special quality whether antique or new. Pierced metal buttons let the fabric underneath peek through. Look for novelty shapes and sizes that will add interest. I don't mind spending extra for good buttons as they add the final sparkle, like the jewels in the crown!

SPECIAL TECHNIQUES

I use buttons in so many different ways. Pearl baby buttons can march along a ribbon or pose as flowers when you highlight them with embroidered leaves and beaded centers. Buttons shaped like flowers and animals can dot a landscape. You can cluster buttons together in mounds or create shapes like paisleys and diamonds.

BUTTON TIPS

- ♪ Keep your dress buttons away from those you use for embellishments. I am constantly coming up short when I need a matched set of garment buttons as I'm always borrowing "one" just for a crazy quilt project.

- ♪ Treat antique buttons like antique lace. Use them in framed pictures, wall hangings, and similar projects that will receive little handling. If you must add them to garments or purses, anchor them with double knots.

- ♪ Before you wash a project, make sure the buttons are up to it.

Detail of a belt (directions, page 113). A collection of buttons from England and Canada are attached with silk buttonhole twist and highlighted with beads.

Sew on your buttons with silk buttonhole twist in a bright color. Come back later and add beads to the buttonholes or stack a small button on top of a large button. Let your imagination run wild and above all have fun.

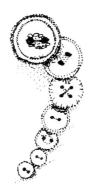

Paisley Shape. Start with the largest button and work down to the smallest button, overlapping slightly as you sew. Use one thread for all, making sure to anchor with a knot behind each button.

Diamond Shape. Start with the largest button in the center and work out in a straight line to the smallest. Repeat on the opposite side. The middle button sits on top, and the others overlap down to the smallest.

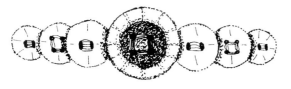

Clusters. Gather a good variety of shapes and colors. Start in the center with a shank button (one that is taller). Keep adding assorted buttons under the shank button, fanning out to the smallest buttons. Use one thread and always knot behind each button.

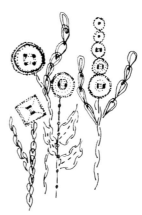

Flowers. Some buttons look just like flowers and all you have to do is add stems and leaves. Choose buttons with four holes and add colorful beads to the centers. Use some buttons in rows and some singly. Now work stems and leaves in outline stitch and chain stitch. Come across the stems with a ribbon bow.

Detail from the "Exotic Gypsy Escapade" crazy quilt weskit. Charms and doodads highlight silk ribbon embroidery.

Anchor buttons. Use buttons to anchor ribbons into place. They are perfect in corners where seams meet or a ribbon crosses over a piece of lace. You can also collage them over lace to help tack it down.

CHARMS AND DOODADS

Remember the charm bracelets we all wore in the Sixties? I took mine apart two years ago and sewed the charms onto a Victorian Christmas wreath. Ever since then, I've been adding charms to all my work. Charms can be expensive, so I look for them in dime stores, bead shops, and hobby stores (the miniature sections are good sources).

I've also discovered other tiny tokens—leaves, cupids, hearts, hands, scissors—that are made of metal, plastic, glass, and mother-of-pearl. For want of a better word, I've come up with the name "doodads." (My Japanese students refer to them as doo-dahs!) Mixed with buttons, doodads finish off the crazy quilt piece. Highlight them over a folded ribbon or center a few in a special pendant. Be careful, for doodads are addictive!

SMOCKING AND FABRIC MANIPULATION

In my crazy quilt landscapes, I don't just "paint" with the fabrics. I "sculpt" with them, twisting and folding them to create texture and depth.

Smocking. I do my smocking by hand and keep it very free-form to achieve textures. To prepare the fabric, hand-baste in rows using evenly spaced running stitches. The rows should be about ¼" (6 mm) apart. Pull the threads, adjust the gathers, and fasten each thread end in a knot at the edges. Now, embroider over the gathers using horizontal or diagonal stitches. Try using silk ribbon or silk threads. You can also be highlight with beads. Remove the holding stitches once you've finished.

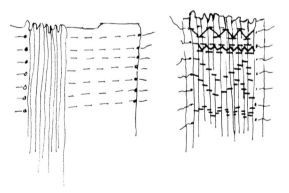

Pleating. Use this simple pleating technique to create the look of field rows. Evenly fold the piece of fabric into ¼" (6 mm) folds. Baste the folds in place and steam-press. Treat the pleated piece as a flat piece of cloth and sew it directly into the foundation.

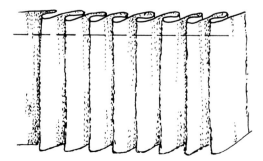

Ruching. The Victorian women loved the look of ruching and, of course, overdid it. In crazy quilt landscapes, the ruched fabric gives a soft, pleated look. Run basting stitches on either side and gather up. Now sew by machine along the edges to hold the folds in place.

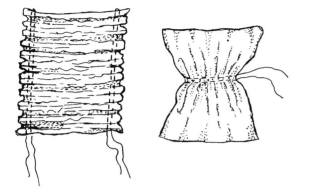

Burned Edges. Thanks to Yvonne Porcella, I've learned how to burn the edges of silk with a candle—and I haven't looked back! In fact, all types of fabric can be distressed in this fashion. Any fabric with polyester will bead along the edge. Cotton is more flammable for a charred look. Silk takes on a lovely brown edge. In fabric painting, hills and mountains with burned edges look natural and dimensional, and I can design a more contemporary piece. Although burned edges are amazingly sturdy, I do not recommend them for garments or articles that will receive lots of wear and tear.

Be sure to work in a safe, ventilated area. Place the candle in a large metal pan. Draw or trace the shape with a white pencil and cut out ¼" (6 mm) beyond the line. With a steady hand, hold the fabric to the flame and burn to the drawn edge. Silk smells like burning chicken feathers, so warn the family before you begin! Cotton will flame up, so use caution.

Wrinkled Fabric. I'm very good at this technique! On one occasion, out of sheer frustration, I slammed the iron down on a piece that was to be a soft rolling hill. When I raised the iron, all the wrinkles had flattened out into interesting creases and folds. I used it "as is" and embellished it with beads and embroidery stitches.

For "planned" wrinkles, try this: Dampen the fabric and scrunch it up into a smaller size. Iron with a medium iron directly on top. The fabric can be fused from the back with iron-on interfacing and worked into crazy quilting or fabric pictures.

LACE, DOILIES, AND HANKIES

Lace is a very personal embellishment—either you love it or you don't. If you do love lace, don't be shy. The Victorian penchant for always overdoing a good thing gives us permission to add lots of it!

In the collage process, lace is a layer of accent and texture. White lace on pastel foundations gives a soft, feminine look; black lace on jewel tones adds drama. Lace can act as a base for buttons, beads, and doodads. Long, narrow laces can accent seams (tack down both sides with Nymo thread). You can decorate lace with embroidery stitches, beads, and small buttons for extra sparkle.

Reserve your heirloom lace for special pictures, wall hangings, and similar projects that will not receive lots of wear and tear. The monetary and/or sentimental value of your lace will determine if you can cut into it. (For a closer look at lace types, see Findings.)

An Australian scene in the making shows burned silk and rayon. The fabric in the foreground has been wrinkled with an iron and sewn into place. The finished piece can be seen on the wall in Photo 33.

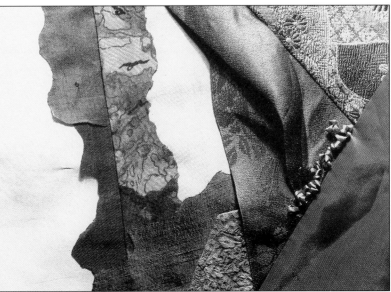

A Lacy Story

I have a theory about using heirloom lace that I preach to all my classes. "Why keep these sentimental things hidden away in drawers? What are you saving them for? Your children, who will toss them out as Mother's old junk? Do you want some other quilter to find them at the Goodwill to use and treasure?" One day at the Houston Quilt Show, I was really on the soap box and gave them a good lecture—which I promptly forgot about until I received a letter from a student in Texas two months later.

It seems this particular student was the eldest of four sisters. When their mother died, she was made the executor of the will. The mother, in her infinite wisdom, willed all the lace heirlooms to the oldest daughter. No matter how hard this daughter tried, she could not convince the other sisters that she, as the executor, had not made that decision herself! Now you must realize that Southerners love lace and use it a great deal, and this lady was not about to share it with her sisters. After all, Mama wanted her to have it!

This incident caused a huge family rift, and the sisters did not speak to each other for four years. After my class, the eldest sister had a lot to think about, because she had all Mama's lace folded up in plastic bags in an old hope chest. She went through all the pieces and, after saying a prayer and asking Mama's forgiveness, began cutting up the doilies, handkerchiefs, and lace trims. She proceeded to create four exquisite crazy quilt collages, with names, dates, and all kinds of family memorabilia. They were beautifully matted and framed. She then called all the sisters together for a "truce dinner" and presented each one with a picture.

Needless to say, they all cried and made up. Each sister now has her own family treasure to admire, a remembrance of dear old Mama, who caused all the trouble in the first place!

water. Keep repeating until the stain is gone, and rinse after each application. Of course, if all else fails, you can cut around the age spots or hide them under mounds of buttons, ribbon roses, and beads!

Tea Dyeing. I use white lace only with pastel projects. Most often, I use antique cream-colored lace. The easiest way to age lace or to camouflage age stains in old lace is to tea-dye it. I'm not above brewing myself a cup of tea and inserting clean lace. I pull out my nicely dyed lace when the cup is finished! (It also works with coffee if you're desperate. Many times my students have "saved" a piece of crazy quilting by dunking harsh white lace into their coffee cups!) After a thorough rinsing, the lace is rolled in a paper towel to catch the excess moisture and ironed dry.

DOILIES

Small doilies—round or oval—can be used whole or cut into half-circles or corner fan shapes for special effects. Just make sure the raw edges are hidden in seam lines. If a seam is less than perfect, layer on a doily! Embellish further with beads and ribbon roses.

ANTIQUE LACE
(AND ANTIQUE LOOK-ALIKES)

Cleaning. Old lace and hankies can be unusable because of stains. The best way to clean them is to wash in a mild detergent, rinse thoroughly, and lay them out on the grass to dry in the sun. The theory is that the chlorophyll in the green grass helps bleach out the stains. If this fails, try using diluted bleach on the stains. Rinse carefully and wash the lace again. Be aware that bleach weakens the fibers.

Age spots can be soaked clean in a mixture of 1 cup buttermilk, ½ teaspoon vinegar, and 4 cups

A melange of laces highlights a piece of crazy quilting. A fancy embroidered hankie peeks out from behind a Battenberg doily and a section of antique crochet edging. To the left is a tatted medallion.

Lace Fan

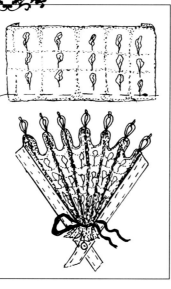

Anne Whitsed of Brisbane, Queensland, Australia shares a lovely design for a lace fan. Cut a piece of lace about 2" (5 cm) long. Gather one edge tightly and tack it down onto the fabric. Cover the raw edges with ribbon and embellish with beads.

HANKIES

Use the lace edge of hankies or the whole corner of an embroidered hankie for crazy quilting. Sew the cut edge into a seam and let the fancy corner overlay the fabric. Initialed hankies from family and friends can personalize a piece. Many handkerchiefs can be "photo-finished." Try adding grandma's photo to an antique hankie . . . better yet if it belonged to her!

RIBBONS

Crazy quilting would not be the same without ribbons. From polyester to silk, the variety is staggering. The widest ribbons can be sewn down as cloth pieces or made into campaign ribbons with a photographs. French moiré ribbons add a quaint Victorian look. Metallic and printed ribbons add contemporary glitter and design. Spark organdy is a lustrous see-through ribbon. Polyester ribbon floss can be used for punch needle, traditional Victorian embroidery, and ruching.

Japanese silk ribbon is a charmer, and I use it as much as possible. It is extremely pliable and comes in over one hundred colors. Most amazing is its versatility. As embroidery thread, it adds texture and dimension (see Ribbon Embroidery). As a free-form embellishment, it can meander and twist over the crazy quilt surface, take shape as beautiful, three-dimensional flowers, or hang loose as tassels.

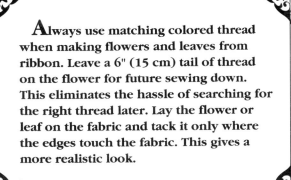

Always use matching colored thread when making flowers and leaves from ribbon. Leave a 6" (15 cm) tail of thread on the flower for future sewing down. This eliminates the hassle of searching for the right thread later. Lay the flower or leaf on the fabric and tack it only where the edges touch the fabric. This gives a more realistic look.

Ribbons and buttons create a nosegay. The stems are worked with silk buttonhole twist in stem stitch and featherstitch.

ROSES

Concertina Rose. Thread up with a knotted matching thread first. The size of the rose varies, depending on the width of the ribbon. For a medium ½" (12 mm) ribbon, cut a 12" (30 cm) length; for wider ribbon, use a longer length. Fold the ribbon at a right angle in the center (a). Bring the ribbon on the bottom up and over (b). Look for the new ribbon on the bottom and fold it up and over (c). The folds will take on a square look (d). Simply keep folding from right side, to top, to left side, to bottom until you've used up the ribbon (about twenty times). Grasp the two ends in one hand and let go of the folded ribbon. It will spring out in accordion folds! (Remember our nursery school Christmas chains, or the drink straw covers we folded into accordion lengths?) Hold the two ribbon ends loosely in one hand. With the free hand, gently pull down one ribbon (it doesn't matter which one) until a rose is formed. Using the needle with knotted matching thread, go down through the center of the rose and come up again to tack it into place. Do this two or three times, finishing on the bottom. Now, wring its neck! Simply wind the thread tightly around the bottom, make a slip knot, and cut the thread about 6" (15 cm) from the flower (e). You'll attach the rose with this thread end later. Now, carefully cut the two ribbon ends off as close to the base as possible.

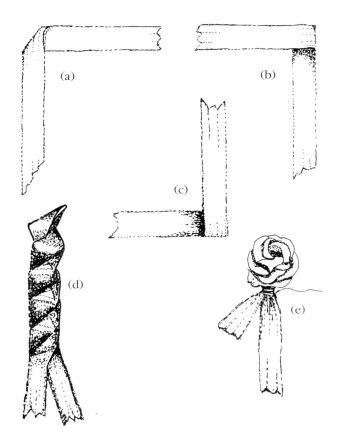

Folded Rose. This rose takes practice, but it is worth the effort. Cut a 10" (25 cm) length of ¾" (18 mm) satin ribbon. Fold one end down at a right angle (a). This will be the center of your rose. Hold this end in one hand just below the fold and grasp the extending ribbon with the other. Twist and fold out; do not pull tight (b). Become looser at the outer edges (c). Keep twisting and folding until you are satisfied (d). With a matching thread, run the needle through the bottom and tack tightly. Cut off excess at the bottom.

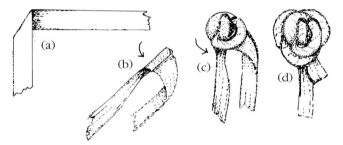

Free-Form Flowers. These gathered flowers are very free-form. Please remember that no two flowers are ever alike in a garden, so just relax and have fun! For tiny flowers, use a narrow ribbon (⅛", ¼", 2 mm, or 4 mm) cut in 3" (8 cm) lengths. For ½" to 1" ribbon (up to 2.5 cm), cut 4" (10 cm) lengths. Fold both ends and baste along one long edge (a). Gather tightly and knot. Whipstitch the folded ends together (b). Leave a tail for sewing on later.

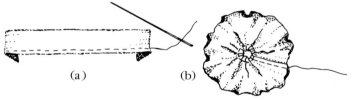

Gathered Ribbon Roses. These roses are wrapped and gathered for a softer look. Cut a ¾" (18 mm) ribbon about 4" (10 cm) long. Lay it down flat and turn both ends down at right angles. Run a gathering stitch along the bottom edge (a). Pull the thread to gather and make a knot. Now wrap the ribbon around and around (b). Stitch the bottom of the rose tightly and cut off the dangling ends. Leave a 6" (15 cm) tail. Try these ribbons in spark organdy or lace.

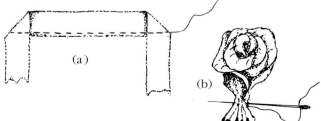

Wire Ribbon Roses. Silk and polyester ribbons now come with a thin wire edge. The wire can be twisted and manipulated into wonderful shapes such as wrapped roses. Cut ¾" (18 mm) ribbon about 8" (20 cm) long. Turn one end at a right angle (a). Now simply twist and fold, turn the rose and twist and fold, until the rose looks full. Turn the outer edge at a right angle and sew up the bottom (b). With a knotted thread, anchor the bottom by going down through the top and then through the sides, leaving a 6" (15 cm) thread. You can make this rose with regular ribbon too.

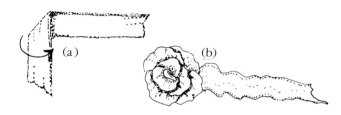

Ribbon Leaves. Leaves can be made from ribbon ⅛" to 2" wide (up to 5 cm), depending on the size of the flower. Cut a 1" (2.5 cm) ribbon 1½" (4 cm) long and fold it into a prairie point. Baste along the wide edge (a). Pull the thread to gather (b). Make a knot and leave a tail for tacking (c). Remember, leaves are tacked down first, then the flower!

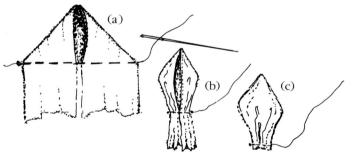

RUFFLES AND BOWS

Ribbon Bows. Ribbon bows can be folded into place at seam intersections and tacked down with buttons or beads. You can pull up a length of ribbon that is woven through lace and form a bow. Or gather several narrow ribbons to form one loop; anchor down with buttons or beads and fluff out the loops. Use ribbon bows to highlight special charms and doodads.

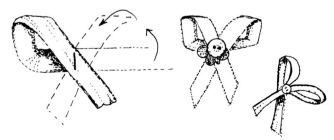

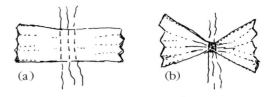

Anne Whitsed's Ribbon Fans

Use 1½" (4 cm) ribbon that is firm enough to hold a crease. Cut a 5" (13 cm) length and fold one end ¼" (6 mm) to the wrong side. Finger-press and fold again. Fold the ribbon accordion style (a). Fold the remaining end to the wrong side. Stitch together at one end. When sewing down, decorate the touching folds with embroidery and beads (b).

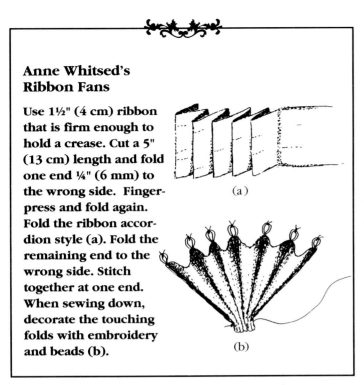

(a)

(b)

Ribbon Ruching. Take running stitches on both sides of a ribbon ½" to 2" (12 mm to 5 cm) wide (a). Pull up both edges so the ribbon gathers into tight pleats (b). Knot the end of the threads and sew into place as a meandering ribbon or seam cover. Decorate further with buttons and beads. Satin, silk, and organza ribbons work well.

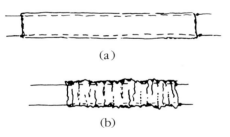

(a)

(b)

Ribbon Ruffles. Ribbon 1½" (4 cm) and wider makes nice ruffles. Run a basting stitch down the center of the ribbon and pull to gather. Highlight the ruffled ribbon by sewing down with French knots or beads.

Ribbon floss can be self-ruffled. Look closely at one end and you'll notice the many threads. Pull one in the middle, gathering up the ribbon in one hand. Now carefully even out the gathers. Tack down with beads or embroidery stitches as a meandering ribbon or seam cover.

Ruched Bows. Use satin or silk ribbon 1½" to 2" (4 cm to 5 cm) wide. Cut a 1" to 2" (2.5 cm to 5 cm) length. Run three gathering lines down the center (a). Pull tight (b).

NOVELTIES

Meandering and Twisted Ribbon. Japanese silk ribbon can decorate a single fabric piece or wander over several. This ribbon is usually 2 mm or 4 mm wide. It is soft and pliable and handles like bias ribbon. As in British crazy quilting, let the ribbon wander across the base work to add texture and color. Tack down with French knots or beads.

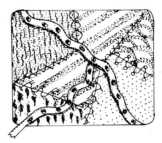

Twisted ribbon is just a bit different because the ribbon is actually twisted at right angles and the angle is anchored down with a bead or French knot. The twisted ribbon can be shaped into bows, hearts, and initials. The twists and French knots should be about ¼" (6 mm) apart.

Ribbon Prairie Points. Ribbon prairie points can be sewn directly into a seam or tucked under ribbon or lace edging. They can be decorated with beads or French knots. Use a ribbon at least 1" (2.5 cm) wide, cut twice the width to form a rectangle (a). Fold down the top corners to the center of the bottom edge to form a triangle. Sew along the bottom (b). For other effects, try sewing two different colored ribbons together or line the ribbon with lace.

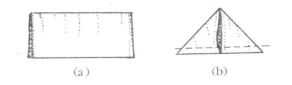

(a)   (b)

Virginia Wright's Prairie Points with Shisha Mirrors

Virginia Wright sent me an embellishment idea that is fun and different. Make a traditional prairie point. Now insert a shisha mirror into the fold. Tack down the point with embroidery stitches. Tack back the fold with catch stitches and beads.

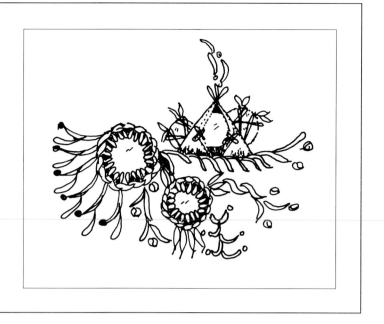

Woven Ribbon. Try weaving ribbon for a checkered look or extra texture. Silk ribbon or very narrow satin ribbon can be woven into various shapes. Lay down a "warp" of horizontal lines, then weave in and out with vertical lines of a different color.

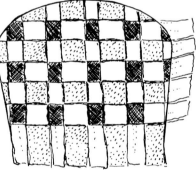

Anne Whitsed of Brisbane, Queensland, Australia, delights in miniature work. Here she has made a silk ribbon basket filled with beads, buttons, and ribbon flowers.

CORDS AND TASSELS

Novelty cords are easy to make. Twisted, wrapped, or braided, they can decorate purses, pendants, and belts or be whipstitched as a "frame" around a crazy quilt pillow. Tassels are a fun Victorian decoration for clothing, purses, and small pendants. Often, it's final details like these that make a project look professional instead of homemade.

Braided Cord. A variety of cords combined can give a new look to the traditional braid. Try rattail, embroidery floss, silk ribbon, and metallics. Decide on the thickness wanted and choose complementary cords. Cut 1¾ times the desired length and divide into three groups. Braid tightly or loosely.

Concertina Cord. If you've already tried the concertina rose (page 74), this cord will be easy. Use ribbon up to ¼" (6 mm) wide. Firm satin ribbon works best. Cut a piece of ribbon four times the desired length. Fold in the center at a right angle. The ribbon on the bottom comes up and over and lays across the top. Keep folding the bottom ribbon up and over, holding the folds in the one hand. If the cord is long, let it spring out while you make the last few folds and knot the end. Concertina cords are

a wonderful way to attach doodads and sewing implements to sewing chatelaines (slip the ribbon through an opening on the item before you begin).

Covered Cord. From fabric, cut a bias strip three times the width of a purchased cording core. Cut the cording core twice as long as the bias strip. Fold the bias in half lengthwise, right sides together (you will turn the fabric right side out upon finishing). Sandwich the cord in the fold of bias material (a), with cord and bias even at one end. Stitch, using a zipper foot. When you reach the end of the fabric (at the midpoint of the cord), sew across the fabric and cord (b). Trim the seam closely. Carefully slip the fabric back over the other end of the cord (c), forming a covered tube (d). Great for button loops and Chinese knots!

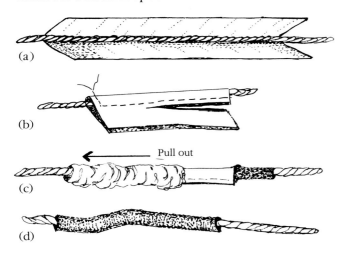

Twisted Cord. This method requires two people, two pencils, and a doorknob! You can twist a variety of yarns and threads together into one cord. Cut each yarn or thread three times the desired length of the twisted cord. Hold all the strands together and tie a knot at each end.

To begin, each person slips a pencil behind a knot. Keeping the yarn taut, twist in opposite directions (a). When the yarn begins to kink (b), catch the center over a doorknob (or hook). Bring the pencils together for one person to hold. The other grasps the center of the yarn and slides a hand down at short intervals, letting the yarn twist (c). When I'm working alone, my "second person" is a nail anchored to the edge of my worktable.

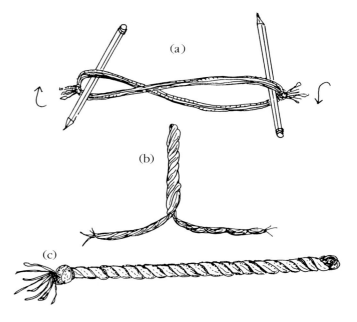

Wrapped Cording. Wrapped cording is easy to make yet looks handsome and expensive. Use it for purse handles, necklaces, frogs, and edging for pouches and pendants. The cord to be covered should be of a loose weave. The wrapping cord can include embroidery floss, Natesh®, silk buttonhole twist, and metallics. Pin the cord to be wrapped to a corkboard or ironing board or tie it to a nail to give a little tension. Place the wrapping cord parallel to the pinned cord. Begin wrapping tightly and evenly, concealing the end of the wrapping cord as you go (a). When you've reached the planned length, lay a darning needle along the cording with the eye in the direction you are wrapping. Wrap over needle and cord for about ¾" (18 mm). Thread the needle with the wrapping thread (b) and pull through to hide and fasten (c). Cut the thread even with the wrapping. Add a new color, concealing the end of the wrapping thread as in the first step. Continuing wrapping with different cords to the desired length (d).

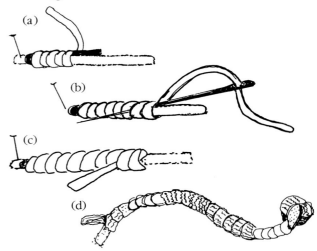

Tassels. Tassels were a favorite adornment for the Victorians. They hung them from velvet curtains, the edges of tablecloths, and pillows. Tassels are easy to make and can be made in any size. For a 4" (10 cm) practice tassel, you'll need a piece of cardboard 4" (10 cm) wide and a thread such as rayon that will hang nicely. Wind the thread around the cardboard—the more thread, the thicker the tassel (a). Use a large darning needle threaded with matching thread to secure the loops at one end (b). Tie securely and leave a tail long enough for attaching to the project later. Clip the other end and remove the cardboard. Now, wrap a neck around the tied end, concealing the ends as for wrapped cording. Use contrasting thread for a special effect (c).

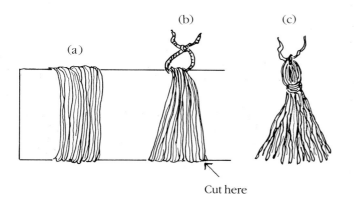

Cut here

You can leave the tassel as is or decorate it further (d). Try adding beads or embroidery to the wrapped portion. Add a cap to the tassel by weaving in and out of the tied top with a contrasting ribbon. Cover the wrapped area of the tassel with lace or fabric. Have fun with tassels!

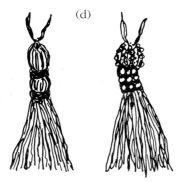

(d)

CHINESE BUTTON BALLS AND FROGS

Try making your own Chinese button balls and frogs with rattail or a heavier cord. These exotic closures can decorate garments and purses and they serve a purpose too.

Chinese Button Balls. For rich-looking balls, use cord ¼" (6 mm) diameter or heavier. Allow up to 10" (25 cm) of cording per button. Hold the cord in the left hand and make a counterclockwise loop (a). While holding the first loop, make another loop above it. Let the excess cord slip under the first loop (b). Weave the excess cord over, under, over, under (c). To tighten, draw up the loops carefully and slowly (d) to make a round ball (e). Cut the cording ½" (12 mm) from the end and sew together. Tuck the sewn ends inside the ball and stitch. Sew on the button immediately, loosely but securely. Wrap the threads around the loose stitches to form a shank (like a metal shank on a commercial button) (f).

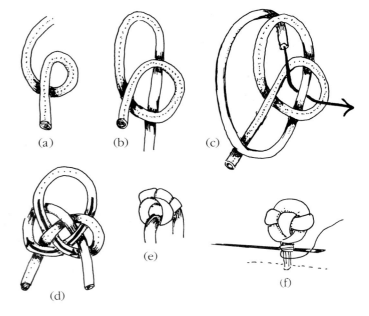

Slip Knot Loop. Cut an 8" (20 cm) length of cording and fold in half (a). Tie a loose slip knot close to the open end (b). Adjust the loop for the button size. Manipulate the knot till it is loose and flat (c) and tack with matching thread. Clip off the ends to ¼" (6 mm) on back and sew down securely. Sew the loop in place with matching thread. This loop is good for purses and garments.

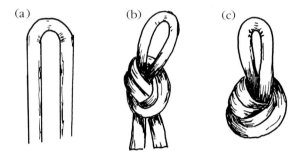

Frogs. Unlike the garden variety, these frogs are used to form ornate closures. For a matched set, one frog will have a Chinese button ball and the other a loop. Choose cording at least 1 yard (.91 m) long for a matched set. Make the Chinese button ball at one end and leave a 2" (5 cm) tail. Bring the long end over to form a loop. Fasten with a thread. Repeat the loops and stitching two more times, to form a three-leaf clover with a ball. You are working on the back side. Turn over and sew the frog to the garment. Form the other half of the frog by following the same loop procedure. This half will have four loops, like a four-leaf clover. One will be the button loop.

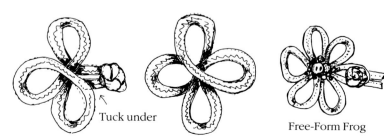

Tuck under

Free-Form Frog

Button Ball Loop. For a decorative loop, proceed to make a Chinese button ball with the chosen cording, but instead of pulling it tight, leave it loose and flat. Turn under the long end to form the loop. Tack it into place with matching thread.

Tuck under and sew in place

Part 3: Projects

The following seventeen projects will start you off on your crazy quilt adventure! All contain actual-size patterns. Photos begin on page 94. Measurements are given in the American system; approximate metric equivalents are in parentheses.

CHATELAINE

This chatelaine is fashioned after a man's tie. It is nice and narrow in the neck portion and feels comfortable to wear. You can work the crazy quilting overall or simply decorate the pockets—they make interesting display areas for sewing treasures, pins, and doodads. The chatelaine is adjustable at the neck seam. It can also be worn as a belt or an actual tie with pockets! It makes for an unusual fashion accessory this way. *Photo P-1*

Size: 4½" wide × 52" long (11 cm × 132 cm); adjust length at neck seam as desired.

Materials & Supplies

- Scraps of fancy fabrics in a variety of solids, patterns, and textures
- ⅓ yard (0.30 m) 44"–45" fancy fabric for backing (½ yard [0.46 m] for pockets-only crazy quilting style)
- ⅓ yard (0.30 m) 44"–45" muslin (6" × 12" [15 cm × 30 cm] piece for pockets-only crazy quilting style)
- 12" (30 cm) square heavy iron-on interfacing
- 6" × 12" (15 cm × 30 cm) Pellon Fleece
- Embroidery floss
- Laces
- Ribbons
- Beads, Nymo thread, and #10 sharps needle
- Buttons
- Variety of doodads or pins to decorate chatelaine
- ¼ yard (0.23 m) 1" (2.5 cm) fancy ribbon (folds into bottom seam)
- 5" (13 cm) ¼" (6 mm) Offray satin ribbon for scissor and pencil holder
- ½ yard (0.46 m) ⅛"–½" (3 mm–12 mm) satin or silk ribbon for concertina cord
- 2" × 2½" (5 cm × 6 cm) piece thick felt
- Snap
- Sewing aids to attach to chatelaine, such as scissors, thimble cage, small ruler
- 1½" yards (1.37 m) rattail

Instructions

1. Trace and cut out three pattern pieces. Tape at A's and B's to make one long pattern. Make a separate pattern for pocket front.
2. Decide which style you want—overall crazy quilting or crazy quilt pockets only.
3. For overall crazy quilting: From long pattern, cut two fancy fabric and two muslin.
4. For pockets-only crazy quilting: From long pattern, cut four fancy fabric.
5. For both styles: From pocket front pattern, cut two fancy fabric, two muslin, four iron-on interfacing, and two fleece.
6. Join long pieces at center back neck with ¼" (6 mm) seam.
7. Using fancy fabric scraps, work crazy quilting on muslin pieces. Be sure to use a variety of shapes, solids, patterns, and textures!
8. Embroider each seam with a variety of Victorian stitches. Add lace and ribbon.
9. Fuse the iron-on interfacing to the pocket fronts and backs.
10. Add beads and buttons and doodads.

Assembly:

1. Machine-baste wide ribbon loops to each end of front. Lay large pieces (crazy quilted front and fancy fabric back OR fancy fabric front and back) right sides together. With a ¼" (6 mm) seam allowance, machine-stitch all around, securing ribbons in seam. Leave opening at one end.
2. Turn out and press edges. Whipstitch opening closed.
3. Sew felt piece on one end for needles (a).
4. Construct pocket fronts: For each, stack fancy backing and finished fronts, right sides together. Add fleece to back. Sew up, leaving opening at bottom. Turn out and press.
5. On the back of one pocket, sew on ribbon for scissor and pencil holder (b).
6. Pin pocket without ribbon to end of chatelaine without needle felt. Whipstitch sides and bottom.
7. Pin remaining pocket to chatelaine. Whipstitch in place, leaving opening at one side for easy access to needles. Add a snap closure (c).
8. Attach scissors and sewing utensils with concertina cord (see page 77). Whipstitch rattail around front pockets to cover seams (d).

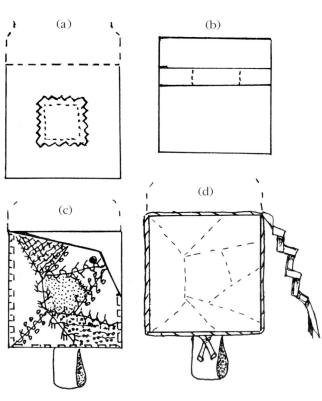

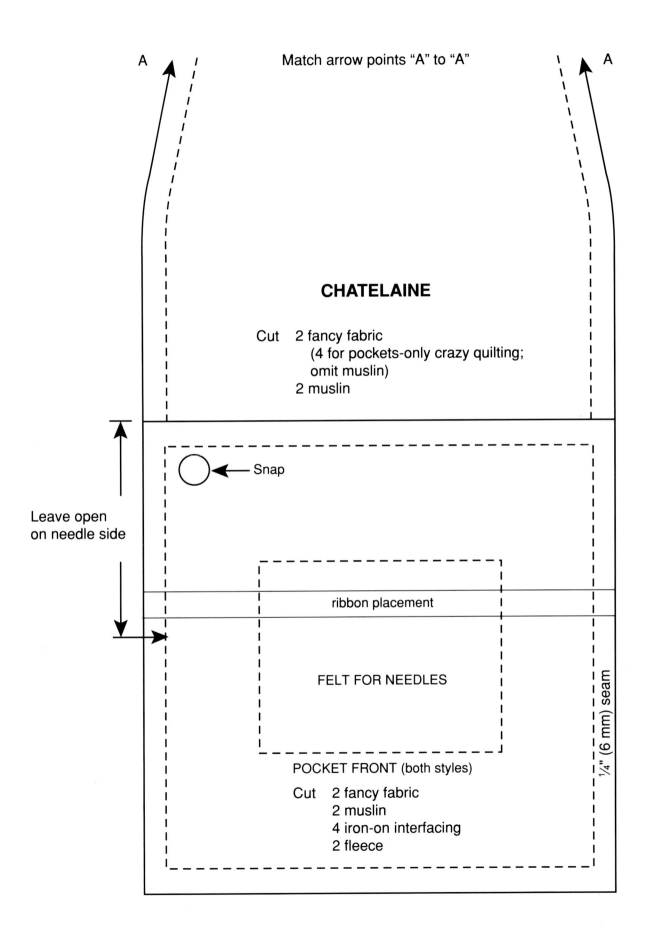

Match arrow points "A" to "A"

A   A

CHATELAINE

Cut   2 fancy fabric
         (4 for pockets-only crazy quilting;
         omit muslin)
        2 muslin

○ ← Snap

Leave open
on needle side

ribbon placement

¼" (6 mm) seam

FELT FOR NEEDLES

POCKET FRONT (both styles)

Cut   2 fancy fabric
        2 muslin
        4 iron-on interfacing
        2 fleece

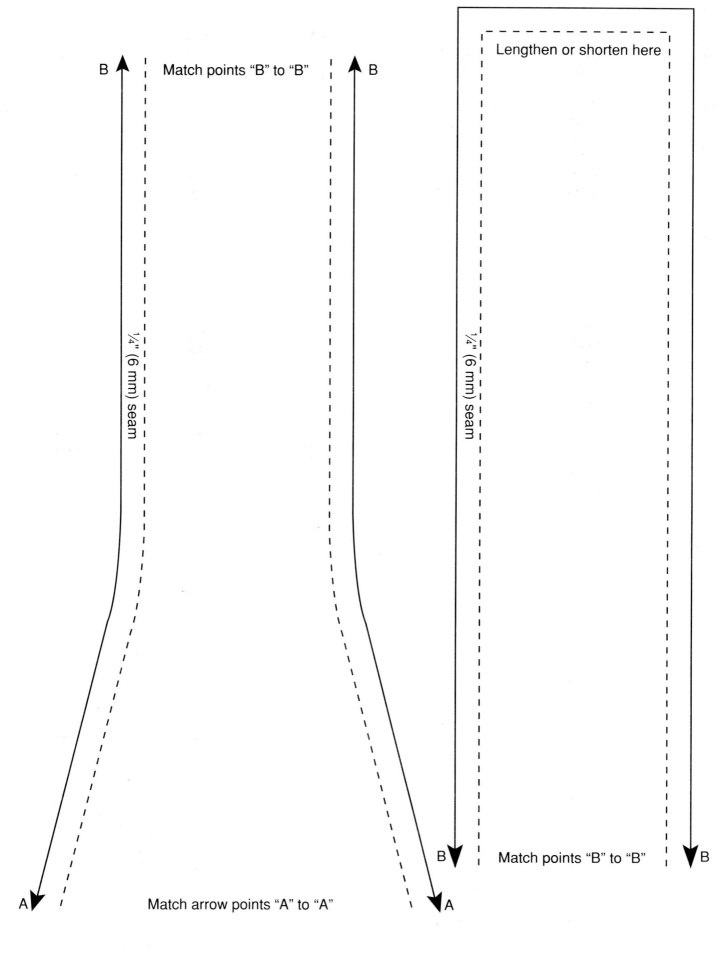

B — Match points "B" to "B" — B

Lengthen or shorten here

¼" (6 mm) seam

¼" (6 mm) seam

B — Match points "B" to "B" — B

Match arrow points "A" to "A"

A — A

SWING PURSES

The swing purse, either circle or rectangle, is an adaptation of the needlecase in *The Crazy Quilt Handbook*. It can be worn around the neck, as a crisscross shoulder bag, or tied to a belt. It makes a very effective fashion statement and will bring lots of attention. By using a variety of cords in the braided strap, you'll get a much more interesting tassel. Decorate the tassel with beads and aluminum Indian dance cones to give a jingle effect. *Photo P-2*

Size: Rectangle purse, 5½" × 6½" (14 cm × 17 cm); circle purse, 6" (15 cm) diameter.

Materials & Supplies

- ◆ Small scraps of fancy fabrics, including a dark solid. Choose satins, silks, cottons, and polyesters if possible; velvets are more difficult to work with
- ◆ 10" × 30" (25 cm × 76 cm) heavy moiré or fancy fabric for lining and backing
- ◆ 9" (23 cm) square muslin
- ◆ 10" × 30" (25 cm × 76 cm) iron-on interfacing
- ◆ 9" × 18" (23 cm × 46 cm) Pellon Fleece
- ◆ Embroidery floss and metallic threads
- ◆ Beads, Nymo thread, and #10 sharps needle
- ◆ Buttons
- ◆ 2½-yard (2.29-m) lengths of assorted cords
- ◆ Large beads
- ◆ Four large buttons
- ◆ 10" × 12" (25 cm × 30 cm) milky template plastic
- ◆ Water-erasable pen
- ◆ Aleene's™ Original Tacky Glue

Instructions

1. Each purse is an exercise in the center piece method (see page 48). Place a small piece of dark fabric in the center of the muslin square. The piece should have at least five angles. Working clockwise (counterclockwise if left-handed), sew down five fat fabric rectangles in turn. After all five pieces are sewn down, cut them into smaller, irregular shapes and begin the next round. Work until the muslin is covered. Press.

2. Decide whether to make the rectangle purse or the circle purse. Place the template plastic on the appropriate pattern and trace on the cutting line. Cut out for a window template.

3. Place the window on the crazy quilting and move it around until you find a design placement that you like. Mark with water-erasable pen, then cut out on marked line.

4. Cover each seam with embroidery stitches. Add special embellishments, such as embroidered initials, a spiderweb, beads, and buttons.

5. Using the window template as a pattern, mark and cut three fancy fabric, four iron-on interfacing, and two fleece.

6. Fuse iron-on interfacing to the back of the crazy quilt and fancy fabric pieces.

Assembly:

1. Lay one fancy fabric piece flat, right side up. Put the crazy quilt piece over it, right side down. Lay a piece of fleece on top. Put one pin in each side to hold the layers together as you work.

2. With a ¼" (6 mm) seam allowance, machine-stitch all around; leave a 2" (5 cm) opening at the center of one end.

3. Trim the fleece ⅛" (3 mm) from the seam to reduce bulk. Turn out and hand-sew the opening closed.

4. Repeat for the back of the purse, layering the remaining backing right side up, lining right side down, and fleece. Press both finished sections.

5. Whipstitch front and back together, up to the points indicated on the pattern.

6. Braid the cords (see page 77) and tie the two ends together in a slip knot. Pull each cord tight to make a neat knot.

7. Lay a narrow bead of glue along the edge and pin the cord in place around the purse, with the tassel hanging at the bottom. Let dry. Whipstitch in place and remove pins.

8. Add large beads to the tassel cords.

9. Sew on large buttons as indicated on pattern.

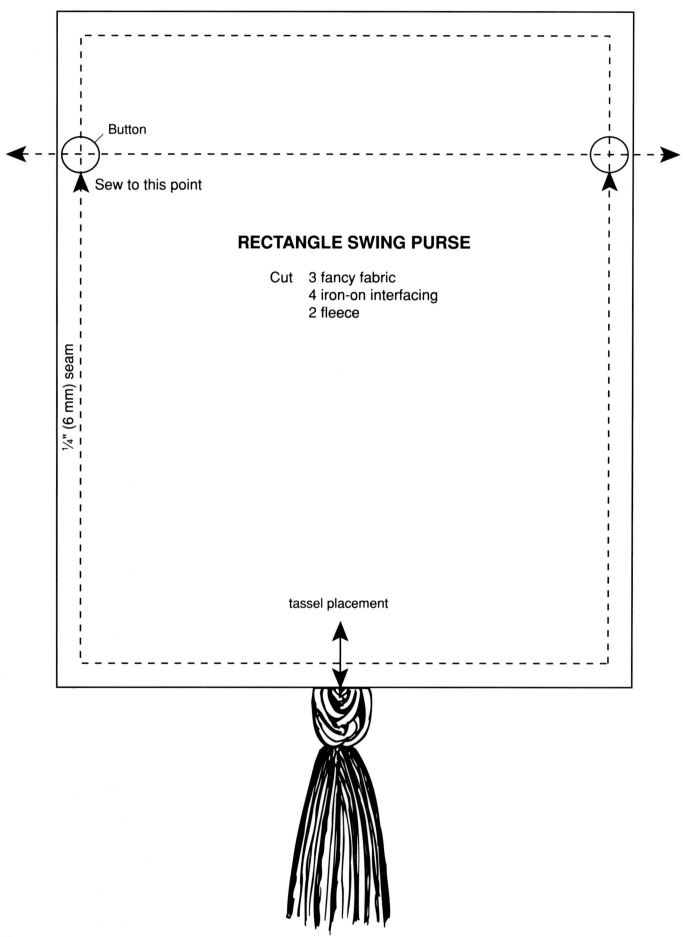

Button

Sew to this point

¼" (6 mm) seam

RECTANGLE SWING PURSE

Cut　3 fancy fabric
　　　4 iron-on interfacing
　　　2 fleece

tassel placement

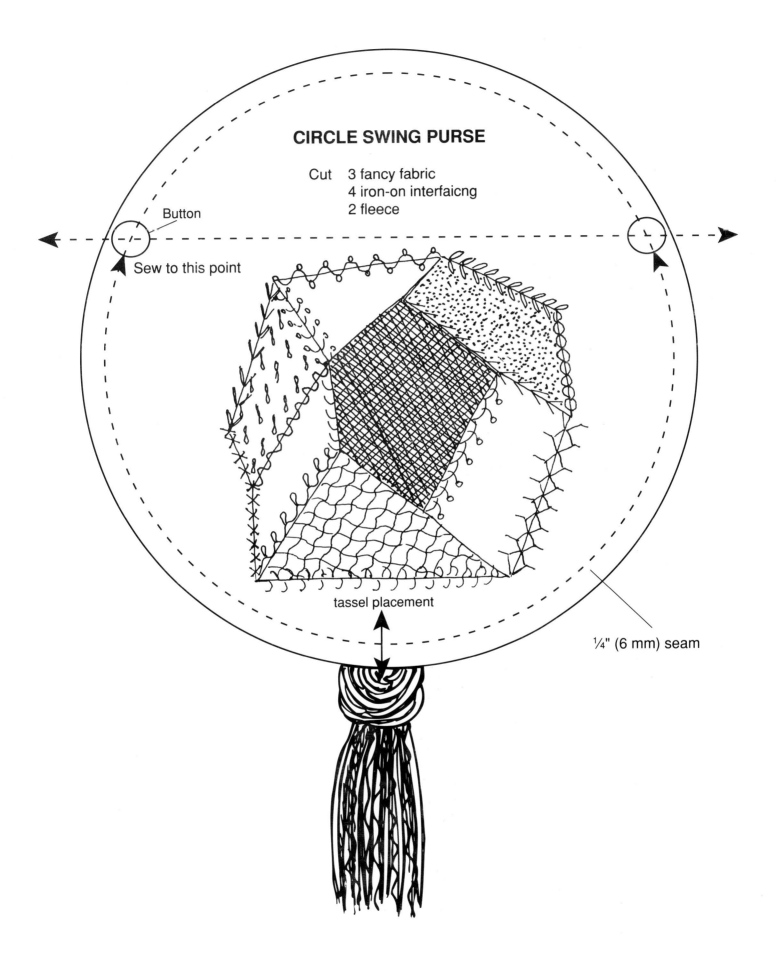

CIRCLE SWING PURSE

Cut 3 fancy fabric
4 iron-on interfaicng
2 fleece

Button

Sew to this point

tassel placement

¼" (6 mm) seam

Half-Circle Purse

One problem with fancy evening bags is that they are just too small. So I've designed a bag that is larger and can be used for both day and evening. For daytime wear, use Ultrasuede and more casual fabrics. Attach a long twisted cord for a shoulder bag. The optional clasp folds over to the fancy fabric side. It can be crazy quilted, embellished with sequins, or left plain. Inside, you can add compartments. *Photo P-3*

Size: 6½″ high × 13" across (17 cm × 33 cm)

Materials & Supplies

- Variety of fancy fabrics
- 9" × 16" (23 cm × 41 cm) fancy fabric for backing (extra for plain clasp)
- ¼ yard (0.23 m) 44"–45" lining fabric
- 9" × 20" (23 cm × 51 cm) muslin
- ½ yard (0.46 m) 44"–45" heavy iron-on interfacing
- ¼ yard (0.23 m) 45" Pellon Fleece
- Embroidery floss
- Laces
- Ribbons
- Beads, Nymo thread, and #10 sharps needle
- Buttons and doodads
- Velcro® fastener

OR

- Snap

- 3 yards (2.75 m) each of three rattail cords for edging (7 yards [6.37 m] to include shoulder strap)
- 10" × 27" (25 cm × 69 cm) milky template plastic
- Large darning needle and heavy thread
- Aleene's Original Tacky Glue

Instructions

1. Place the template plastic on the purse pattern. Trace the cutting and fold lines, then turn the template plastic over, align fold lines, and trace again to complete the half-circle pattern. If clasp is desired, trace it on template plastic also. Cut out template plastic patterns.
2. From half-circle pattern, cut one fancy fabric backing, two lining, one muslin, four iron-on interfacing, and two fleece.
3. From clasp pattern, cut one lining, one muslin, two iron-on interfacing, and one fleece. For plain clasp, cut one fancy fabric backing instead of one muslin. *(continued on page 97)*

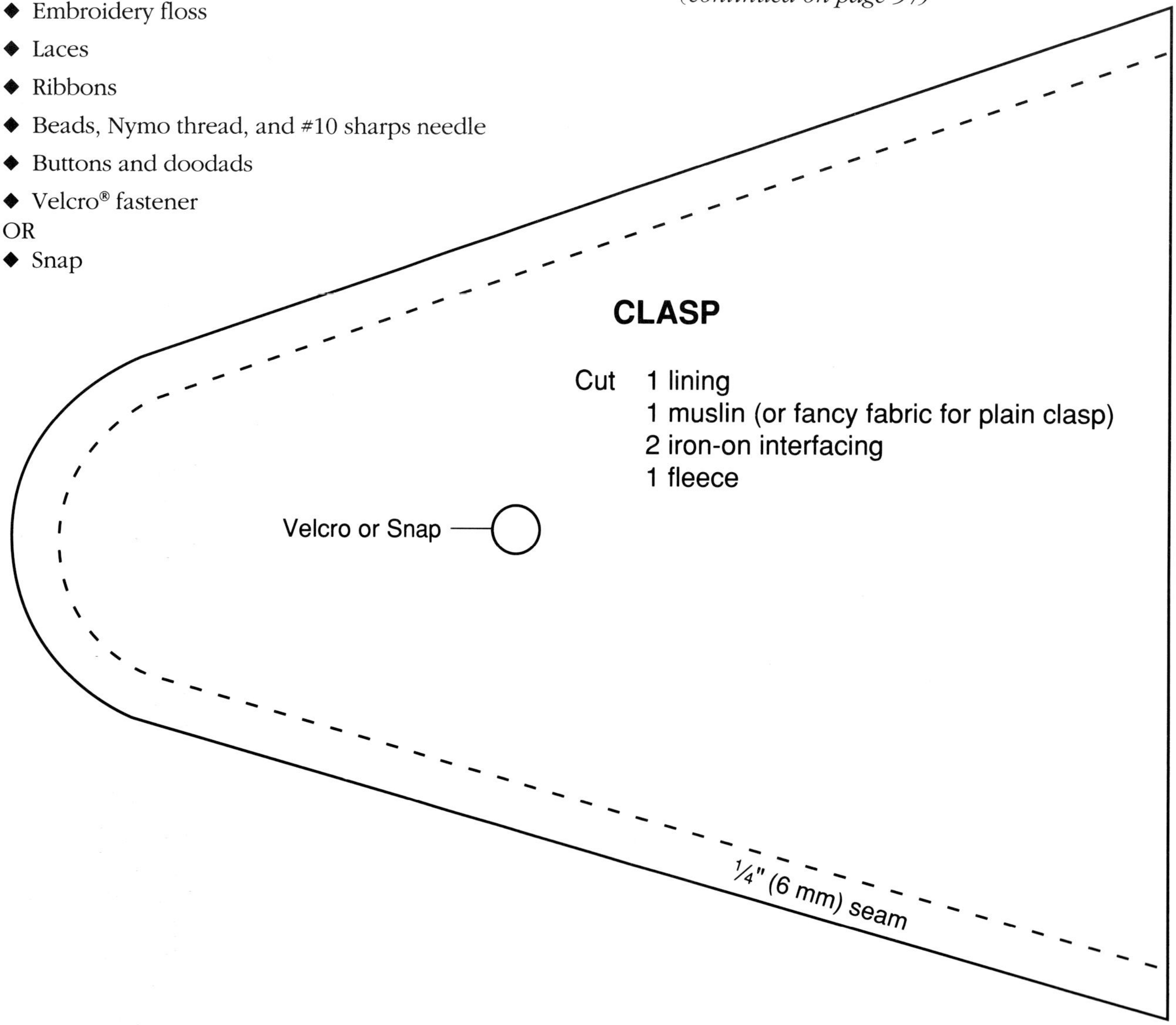

CLASP

Cut 1 lining
      1 muslin (or fancy fabric for plain clasp)
      2 iron-on interfacing
      1 fleece

Velcro or Snap ———○

¼" (6 mm) seam

25. Vest by Wendy Saclier, a well-known Australian quilter and teacher whose embroidery work is spectacular. On this vest, she incorporates Australian wildflowers throughout the piece. Wendy's work is so exact and the fabrics so carefully chosen, the vest takes on an antique look. Modelled by daughter Ele.

PHOTO: MICHAEL SACLIER

26. Masako Ohishi of Tokyo, Japan, is a prizewinning quilt artist who specializes in crazy quilting and embellishments. Here she wears a cocktail ensemble that includes hat, cummerbund, and a heart-shaped purse. Shiny buttons, beads, and doodads add the glitz! With Masako is Keiko Yoshida in a traditional kimono. These two friends often collaborate on quilts.

STUDENTS AND FRIENDS

Here are some of the many wonderful people and inspiring ideas Judith Montano has encountered during her crazy quilting odyssey.

27. "Freedom Coat" by Shirley Fowlkes of Dallas, Texas. Shirley believes clothing should make you feel "free as the birds to fly away seeking new adventures…" Her coat is a purchased ice-washed denim duster decorated with appliqué, embroidery, embellishment "for the sake of embellishment," and painting. Silkscreened, vintage, and new fabrics cover the yoke. The pattern at the hem, called Two Grey Hills, is frequently found on Navajo rugs. Surface embellishments include ethnic jewelry, antique buttons, beads, sequins, milagras, fetishes, and sterling silver buttons. Kanagawa silk ribbon makes the embroidery really stand out. Shirley had to use pliers to pull the needle through the layers of fabric and denim! Modelled by Jane Crutcher.

PHOTO: BARBARA OLIVER HARTMAN

28. "Masako's Camelia" by Masako Ohishi is a mixed media quilt combining embroidery, crazy quilting, and pieced work. The design explodes into shafts of light for unusual motion and vitality. This award-winning piece appeared in the 1990 Flower Exposition in Osaka sponsored by Quilt National.

29. Keiko Yoshida, a quilt teacher and art garment designer, wears her belt and purse on a shopping trip in the Kuramae (wholesale) district of Tokyo. The author loves to shop in Tokyo— "as long as Masako and Keiko are with me!" The threesome travel hand in hand, juggling crowds on the subways, to search for their mutual passion—more fabric!

30. "Flower Picture of Spring and Fall" by Machiko Miyatani. An award-winning quilt shown in the 1990 Flower Exposition in Osaka sponsored by Quilt National. Machiko Miyatani is a famous Japanese quilter whose work evolves from traditional crazy quilting.

31. *Yasako Kurachai teaches quilting in and around Denver, Colorado, and Tokyo, Japan, and has published quilting how-to books in Japanese. Here, she wears one of her contemporary kimono suits adapted from the traditional kimono design. Her drawstring purse has a crazy quilt insert. Anna Huckabay joins her in a child's kimono.*

PHOTO: BILL O'CONNER

32. *Jane Weingarten tried her hand at crazy quilt yarmulkes on the occasion of her son Jed's Bar Mitzvah. Here, Jane, Jed, her husband Peter, and Jamie enjoy a quiet moment together in their backyard .*

34. *An original prom dress designed by Ellen Saucier-Caillouet of Lafayette, Louisiana, for her daughter Angela. The dress features a weskit sleeve and a low-cut neckline and is heavily embellished with lace and beads. The beaded purse is by Tokuko Udagawa. The escort's cummerbund and bow tie, made by the author, are heavily embroidered with silk ribbon. Modelled by Madeleine Montano and Jason Montano.*

PHOTO: BILL O'CONNER

33. *Donna McIntyre of Livingston, Texas, worked a wide band of cotton fabric and lace crazy quilting on a long denim skirt. Outfit is completed with a matching cummerbund and the author's ribbon-embroidered pin. Modelled by Jane Mueller at Ragtime/An Eclectic Collection, Castle Rock, Colorado. The crazy quilt landscape on the wall, "Memories Down Under," is a collage of Aussie fabrics and memorabilia from the author's 1989 trip; shown courtesy of W. Lober.*

PHOTO: BILL O'CONNER

36. Charlie in his horse blanket—a special blanket for a special horse! It was Elizabeth Brown's first project after her first crazy quilting class!

35. Garlands of silk ribbon flowers swirl around silk pillows and a wool baby's blanket. A painted cottage is surrounded by a silk ribbon garden. Ribbon embroidery can create lavish, three-dimensional flowers as seen in these examples from Anne's Glory Box, Newcastle, New South Wales, Australia.

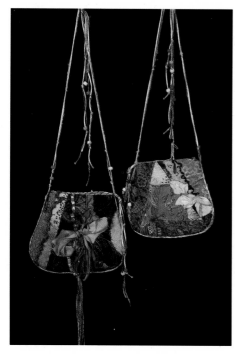

37. Virginia Wright of Norfolk, Virginia, assembled unusual fabrics, then added dimensional embroidery and scrunched "bows" for her urn-shaped purses. Virginia is always sure to inspire new ideas, like her padded butterflies and prairie points decorated with shisha mirrors.

38. Crazy quilt boxes, heart pendants, and a buckle made by students from Anne's Glory Box, Newcastle, New South Wales, Australia. The lids are heavily padded to give a dimensional look. The boxes are from Tennessee Wood Crafters (see Source Guide).

39. *A wall hanging by Virginia Gray inspired by a pattern in* The Crazy Quilt Handbook. *Virginia worked the entire foundation on a whole cloth piece, then cut it down to three smaller shapes, including the center diamond, to make for easier handling during the embellishing. She reassembled the entire piece with nineteenth century French needle-made lace. Read more about Virginia's lavish applications in the Embellishments chapter.*

Photo Courtesy Virginia Gray

40. *Carol Lane's "Kinkoko-ji" ("Japanese Garden in Kyoto") is a beautiful collage of fall colors and memories. Carol Lane is an art garment designer who specializes in punch needle and machine embroidery. She lives in Mill Valley, California, and Tokyo, Japan.*

Photo: Carol Lane

41. *Suzuko Koseki's crazy quilt could fool an expert. Her traditional squares take on an antique look, but up-close examination reveals Japanese kimono fabrics. This charming quilt is titled "Sichi Go San," which means "Children's Celebration."*

Photo Courtesy Hearts and Hands, Tokyo, Japan

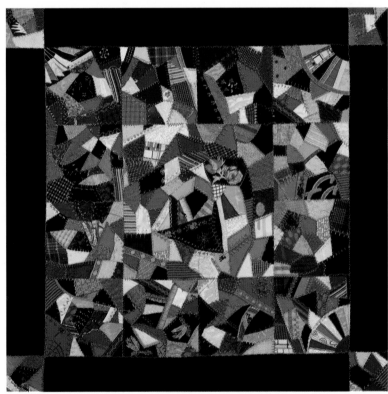

42. *Katsumi Inagaki has produced a traditional-looking crazy quilt that is rich in color and design. The large center piece is surrounded by sixteen squares which in turn are bordered by blank bands. The embroidery is especially detailed.*

Photo Courtesy Hearts and Hands, Tokyo, Japan

PROJECTS

Start crazy quilting!
The author made
most of the projects
pictured here, with a
little help from
students and friends.
Find patterns and
directions in Part 3.

P–1. Chatelaines. Two chatelaines created by Australian students Yvonne Wilcock (blue and yellow) and Normea O'Toole (peacock). On a recent trip, the author challenged her Aussie students: "I'm off for four days. If you finish any projects before I get back, I'll photograph them for a magazine article." Four days later, Normea had finished the chatelaine, two box inserts, a pendant, and a buckle!

P–2. Swing Purses. Swing purses with long cord straps can be worn across the body. The circle purse is decorated with antique beads and buttons. The rectangle purse uses Oriental kimono fabrics and antique Chinese appliqués.

P–3. Half-Circle Purse. Australian students from Anne's Glory Box, Newcastle, New South Wales, made these beautiful half-circle purses. Lee Emlay adorned her version with lampshade fringe and a corded strap.

P–4. Oval Barrette, Pendant, and Buckle. One simple oval inspires three versatile accessories. The barrette is made of Japanese obi fabrics.

P–5. Earrings and Crystal Pouch. Small accessories like these are easy to make with scraps of fabric and Ultrasuede. Ultrasuede edges are burned.

P–6. Ribbon Embroidery Brooches and Floral Pendant. Ribbon-embroidered brooches can be made by the dozen to coordinate with different outfits. The background is drapery weight moire. The circle pendant is a traditional crazy quilt piece overlaid with a spray of concertina and silk ribbon flowers. Miniature quilt by Sally Collins of Walnut Creek, California.

P–7. Christmas Wreath and Victorian Ornaments. Crazy quilt holiday projects decorate a charming vintage shop called Ragtime/An Eclectic Collection in Castle Rock, Colorado.

PHOTO: BILL O'CONNER

P–8. Punch Needle Floral. Flowers made with a large punch needle threaded with ribbon. Stems were made with cotton floss in a three-strand needle. Also shown: A crazy quilt pendant and wooden circular box insert.

P–9. Punch Needle Rooster Purse. A punch needle rooster of Kanagawa silk thread on drapery weight moiré. The finished embroidery piece was assembled into a purse. The small heart pendant and buckle are punched with DMC floss. Heart pendant courtesy Debbie Maul.

P–10. Crazy Quilt Landscapes. The box on the left features a desert scene along the Zane Gray Trail in New Mexico; shown courtesy W. Lober. The other picture is from the author's imagination, but is typical of scenes in the same region.

P–11. Weeping Heart Pendant. An antique cigarette silk featuring the actress Ethel Green highlights a weeping heart pendant. The ribbon and beads are antique. Made for a Denver Art Museum showing. Photographed in Jim Morsicato's garden, Deer Creek Canyon, Colorado.

P–12. Victorian Picture Frame. An elegant frame is pictured amid the finery at Ragtime/An Eclectic Collection in Castle Rock, Colorado. Other crazy quilt project ideas include box and crystal jar covers, brush and mirror backs, a dressing tray insert, and a diary cover.

PHOTO: BILL O'CONNER

P–13. Button-Jeweled Belt. The more buttons and embellishments, the better!

4. Using various fancy fabrics, fill in muslin pieces with crazy quilting.
5. Embroider the seams with Victorian stitches; cover some seams with laces and ribbons.
6. Fuse the iron-on interfacing to the back of the crazy quilting, fancy fabric, and lining pieces.
7. Continue to embellish the crazy quilt piece(s) with beads and buttons. Add doodads and any other embellishments.

Assembly:
1. Lay clasp lining flat, right side up. Put the crazy quilted piece (or fancy fabric piece) over it, right side down. Lay fleece on top. Pin each side.
2. With a ¼" (6 mm) seam allowance, machine-stitch all around; leave straight end open. Turn out and press flat.

3. Following the clasp placement dots, pin clasp to crazy quilted half-circle, right sides together, so that straight edge of clasp extends ½" (12 mm) beyond straight edge of half-circle. Baste in place.
4. Assemble purse halves: Place crazy quilt piece and lining together, right sides together. Place fleece on top. Sew around, making ⅛" (3 mm) seam and leaving 2" (5 cm) open between dots on curved edge. Repeat with fancy fabric, lining, and fleece. Turn both sections and stitch openings closed.
5. With darning needle and heavy thread, whipstitch the two halves together along curved edges. Make twisted cord with rattail and glue along edges; tuck in ends. Attach a longer cord to make a shoulder bag.
6. Fold clasp over to fancy fabric side. Sew on hidden Velcro fastener or snap closure.

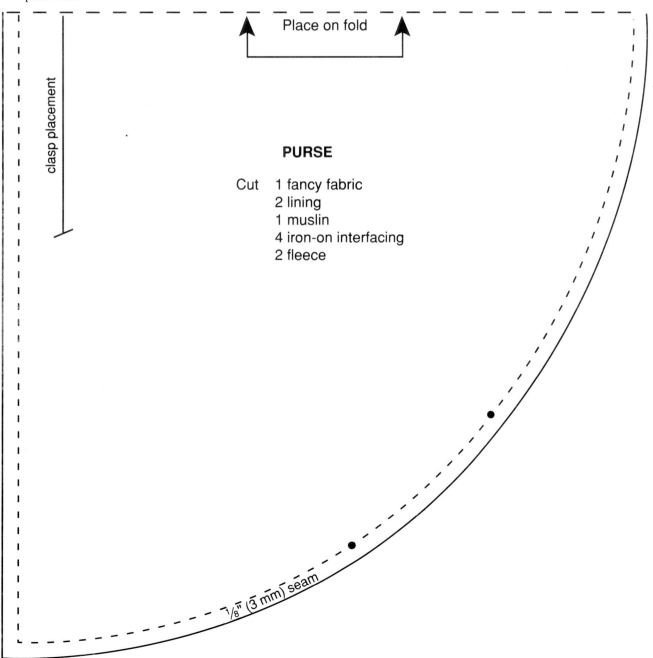

Place on fold

clasp placement

PURSE

Cut 1 fancy fabric
2 lining
1 muslin
4 iron-on interfacing
2 fleece

⅛" (3 mm) seam

Oval Barrette, Pendant, and Buckle

There are so many ways to use crazy quilting. Here is a simple oval shape that can be enlarged or decreased according to your whim. Add a backing to make a soft-sided pouch. I show three variations—a barrette, a pendant, and a belt buckle. *Photo P-4*

Basic oval size for all three projects: 3" × 4½" (8 cm × 11 cm)

Materials & Supplies

For each oval:
◆ Small scraps of six to eight fancy fabrics, including one dark solid
◆ Two 6" (15 cm) squares muslin
◆ 6" (15 cm) square leather backing
◆ 6" × 14" (15 cm × 36 cm) Pellon Fleece
◆ Embroidery floss or silk buttonhole twist
◆ Metallic thread for spiderweb
◆ Beads, Nymo thread, and #10 sharps needle
◆ Buttons and doodads
◆ 6" (15 cm) square art board
◆ 5" × 7" (13 cm × 18 cm) milky template plastic
◆ Large darning needle and heavy thread
◆ Aleene's Original Tacky Glue
◆ Water-erasable pen

For barrette only, add:
◆ Metal barrette clip
◆ Two 15" (38 cm) lengths rattail in complementary colors

For pendant only, add:
◆ Three or four 34" (86 cm) cords for neck
◆ Three 17" (43 cm) cords for twisting around oval
◆ Large beads

For buckle only, add:
◆ Two or three 15" (38 cm) lengths rattail
◆ Clip type belt attachment
◆ Belting, to fit around waist
◆ Fabric to cover belting

Instructions

1. Place template plastic on oval pattern and trace. Cut out for window template.
2. Using window template oval as a pattern, cut one muslin, three fleece, one art board, and one leather.
3. Place small piece of dark fabric in the center of the remaining muslin square. The piece should have at least five angles. Working clockwise (counter-clockwise if left-handed), sew down five fat fabric rectangles in turn. After all five pieces are sewn down, cut them into smaller, irregular shapes and

begin the next round. Work until the muslin is covered. Press.

4. Place the window template on the crazy quilting and move it around until you find a design placement that you like. Mark with water-erasable pen, then cut out ½" (12 mm) outside marked line. (This allowance is turned to the back; see pattern.)
5. Embroider each seam with decorative stitches. Add special embellishments, such as embroidered initials, a metallic spiderweb, beads, and buttons.

Assembly:

1. Starting from the bottom, stack muslin, art board, three fleece, and crazy quilted ovals. The crazy quilted oval will be a bit larger than the others. Turn stack over.

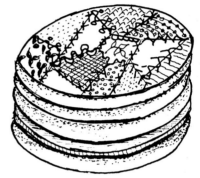

2. With large needle and heavy thread, whipstitch the crazy quilted oval around the fleece and art board. Sew into the bottom muslin. Go around twice; on the second round, stitch deeper into the muslin to pull the assembly taut and even.
3. Spread a heavy layer of glue across the back and affix leather backing.

For Barrette only:

4. Press tightly. Some glue will ooze out. Twist two rattail lengths together and insert one end between crazy quilt piece and backing. Lay rattail around entire edge, making sure glue holds it in place. Tuck in end.

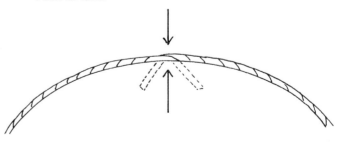

5. Glue the metal barrette clip to the leather backing, bending the barrette to fit the curve of the clip.

For Pendant only:

4. Twist the 34" (86 cm) cords together. Tie a knot in each end, leaving a ½" (12 mm) tail .While glue is still wet, insert the tails of the neck cord between finished oval and backing at points indicated on pattern.

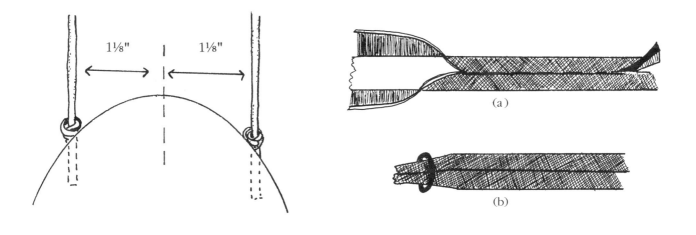

1⅛"   1⅛"

(a)

(b)

5. Press tightly. Some glue will ooze out. Twist the 17" (43 cm) cords together. Place the midpoint of the cords at the top of the oval and pin along edge, making sure glue holds cords in place. Tie the cord ends together in a slip knot at the bottom of the oval. Let the cords dangle and add large beads to the ends. Remove pins when glue is dry.

For Buckle only:

4. Apply twisted rattail edging as for barrette.

5. Make belt: Measure waist and cut belting the same length. Cut the desired fabric 4" (10 cm) longer and 2½ times as wide. Fold fabric over belting and whipstitch closed (a).

6. Glue buckle clip "hook" to back of buckle. Attach to one end of belt. Slip buckle clip "eye" over other belt end (b). Fold over cloth end and stitch in place.

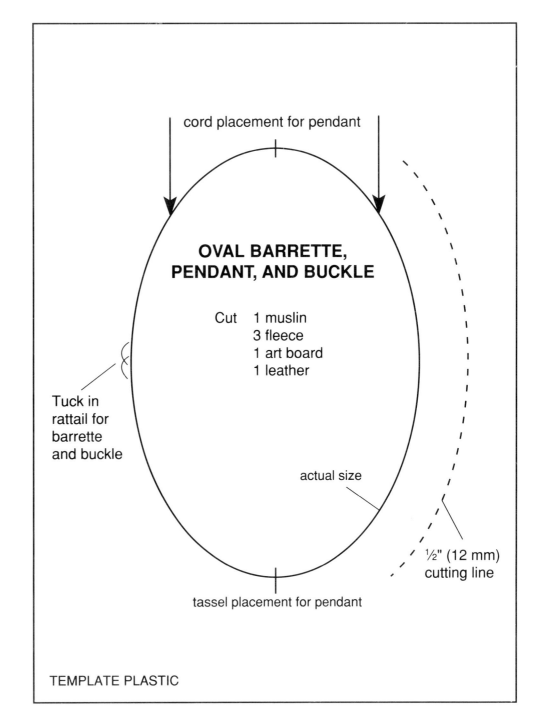

cord placement for pendant

OVAL BARRETTE, PENDANT, AND BUCKLE

Cut 1 muslin
3 fleece
1 art board
1 leather

Tuck in rattail for barrette and buckle

actual size

½" (12 mm) cutting line

tassel placement for pendant

TEMPLATE PLASTIC

CONTEMPORARY EARRINGS

Many times we want large colorful earrings to add zing to our outfits. Ultrasuede fabric is perfect for earrings—it's lightweight and colorfast, and the raw edges will not fray. These earrings are large but very easy to wear! *Photo P-5*

Size: About 2" (5 cm) across.

Materials & Supplies
- Ultrasuede fabric scraps
- 4" (10 cm) square Ultrasuede fabric
- Commercial earring forms, pierced or clips
- Beads
- Doodads
- Good jeweler's glue (must adhere and hold)
- Candle and matches
- Tweezers

Instructions
1. Fold the 4" (10 cm) square of Ultrasuede in half and cut on fold. Now fold the doubled piece in half and cut on fold. You will have four 2" (5 cm) squares.
2. Now decide on the shape (use patterns given or create your own). Stack all four pieces and cut as one.
3. For working, lay the earrings flat in mirror image, that is, opposite to each other.

4. From Ultrasuede fabric scraps, cut out several small shapes. Cut two of each shape and lay them down on the earrings in a mirror image (a).
5. When you are happy with the collage design, singe the edges of the small shapes (see page 71). Light the candle and use the tweezers to hold the pieces close to the flame. Be sure to work in a ventilated area as this step is very smelly. Set aside.
6. Now glue each front to a back, wedging earring form between pieces. For pierced earrings, let the post pierce the back. For clips, cut an X in the back and trim around the metal.

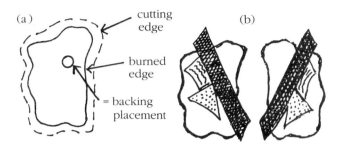

7. Singe earrings around edges (a). Glue the collage pieces to the fronts (b).
8. To place the beads and doodads, you must be brave and loosen up! Simply swirl the glue onto the earring. Lay the earring directly into the dish of beads and press. Quickly add the doodads in along with the beads.
9. Let dry and sign your name on the back.

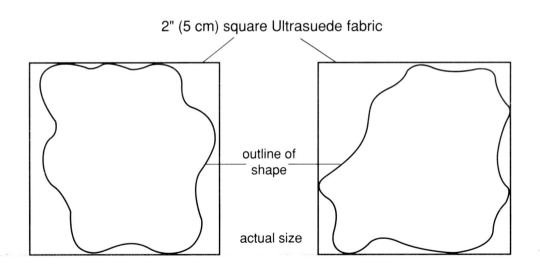

2" (5 cm) square Ultrasuede fabric

outline of shape

actual size

TRADITIONAL EARRINGS

What can be done with all the little pieces of fancy fabric left over from crazy quilting? Make earrings! I save those little scraps, especially the expensive silks, and put them away in plastic bags. The sizes range from 3" square down to 1"! Three to four pieces of fabric per earring is enough. Repeat the fabrics on the second earring, and remember, they are crazy earrings, so they do not have to match! *Photo P-5*

Size: About 1" (2.5 cm) diameter

Materials & Supplies

- ◆ Small scraps of fabric, three or four colors
- ◆ Two 4" (10 cm) squares muslin
- ◆ One 3" (8 cm) square felt
- ◆ Embroidery thread
- ◆ Beads, Nymo thread, and #10 sharps needle
- ◆ Prym® earring forms, clip or pierced (I use size 45, the largest)

OR

- ◆ Covered button forms. Clip off the metal loop in the back and attach commercial earring forms with Krazy Glue® adhesive
- ◆ Aleene's Original Tacky Glue
- ◆ Stain repellant spray
- ◆ Milky template plastic (optional)

Instructions

1. You can use the large circle pattern on this page or the size 45 circle on the the earring form package. Transfer two circles to muslin and cut out.
2. Fill in circles with crazy quilting and embroider each line.
3. Assemble each earring as you would a covered button.
4. Now the earring is ready for beading. Bring the knot up in the back, and bead each line of embroidery. Finish the edges with rounds of beads or let the beads dangle down.

5. Cut out two felt circles and glue to earring backs. Spray earrings with stain repellant.

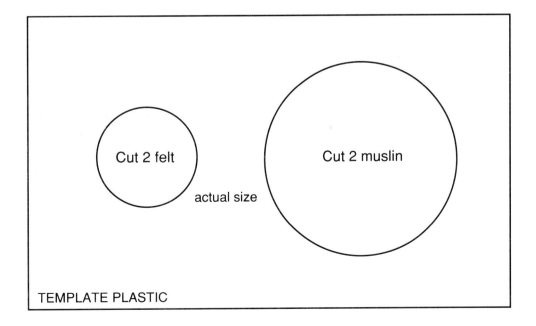

Cut 2 felt

actual size

Cut 2 muslin

TEMPLATE PLASTIC

CHRISTMAS WREATH

Make an heirloom Christmas wreath that will become a family favorite. This simple fabric doughnut is heavily embellished with laces, beads, buttons, and charms. Use silks, velvets, and satins to give a rich luster. *Photo P-7*

Size: 14" (36 cm) diameter

Materials & Supplies

- Scraps of fancy fabric
- 16" (41 cm) square fancy fabric (moiré, satin, velvet) for backing
- ¼ yard (0.23 m) 44"–45" fabric for bow
- 16" (41 cm) square muslin
- Embroidery floss and metallic thread
- Laces
- Satin ribbon, various lengths and widths
- Beads, Nymo thread, and #10 sharps needle
- Buttons
- Charms and Christmas doodads
- Short pieces ¼" ribbon (or 4 mm silk ribbon), various colors
- 1¼ yards (1.14 m) ruffled lace (optional)
- 1¾ yards (1.60 m) rattail
- Polyester stuffing
- 18" × 24" (46 cm × 61 cm) paper for pattern
- 10" (25 cm) square milky template plastic
- Aleene's Original Tacky Glue

Instructions

1. Trace the wreath quarter-pattern onto template plastic and cut out.
2. Fold the large sheet of paper in half. Finger-press. Fold again into quarters. Lay the pattern template in the folded corner, making sure straight edges are flush with folded edges. Trace onto paper. Cut out and unfold.
3. Using the paper pattern, cut one muslin circle and one fancy fabric backing circle.
4. Fill in the muslin circle with crazy quilt base work. Be sure to press every piece of fabric as you go and cut out from behind every seam.
5. Lay down laces and ribbons. Hold in place with tacky fabric glue, then tack down with thread.
6. Embroider remaining seams with Victorian stitches. Be sure thread is a bright contrasting color. You want the stitches to show!
7. Embroider any special initials or extras now.
8. Highlight the laces and ribbons with the beads (use them in place of French knots).
9. Add buttons and doodads. Highlight each one by sewing it to a loop of ¼" (6 mm) ribbon.

Assembly:

1. If you want a ruffled lace edge, pin it to wreath now, right sides facing and edges matching.
2. Lay finished circle and fancy backing circle right sides together and pin.
3. With a ¼" (6 mm) seam allowance, machine-stitch all around the outer edge (catching lace ruffle in seam). Leave a 4" (10 cm) opening (a).
4. Turn out and sew the inner circle by hand (b). Stuff wreath tightly and whipstitch opening closed.
5. Cover the inner and outer seams with rattail. Use embroidery floss to whipstitch over the seams (c). This extra effort really makes the wreath special!

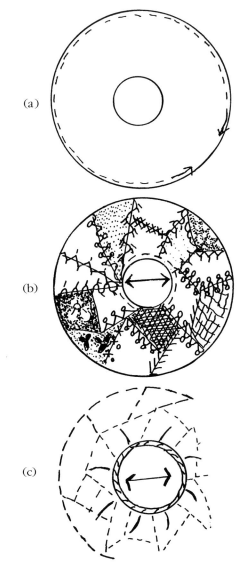

6. Make bow: Cut strip 6 ½" × 43" (17 cm × 109 cm). Fold in half lengthwise, right sides together. Sew raw edges, leaving 4" (10 cm) opening. Turn out and press; stitch opening closed. Tie around wreath.
7. Add a rattail hanging loop to the back.

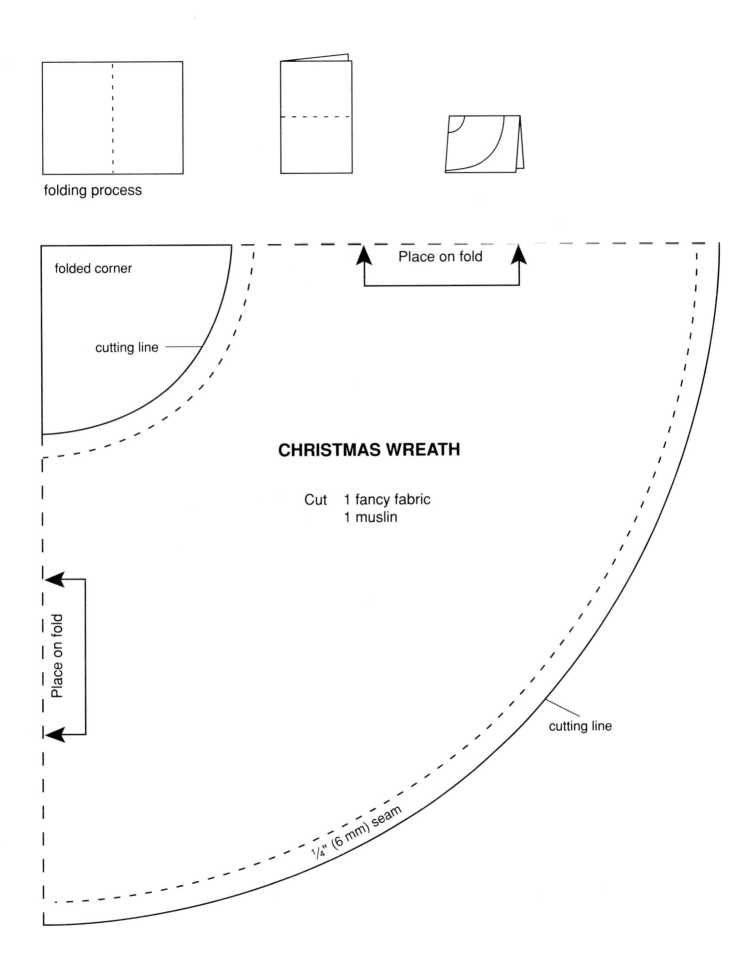

folding process

folded corner

cutting line

Place on fold

CHRISTMAS WREATH

Cut   1 fancy fabric
        1 muslin

Place on fold

cutting line

¼" (6 mm) seam

Victorian Ornaments

Christmas comes every year and much too fast for most of us! Here are four Victorian ornaments sure to become heirlooms. You can also make the heart, basket, or stocking soft, double-sided, and open at the top. What a lovely way to present a special gift! Remember that ornaments can come in a variety of colors. *Photo P-7*

Sizes:

Heart, 3½" × 3¾" (9 cm × 10 cm)
Basket, 3½" × 4½" (9 cm × 11 cm)
Bell, 3¾" × 3¾" (10 cm × 10 cm)
Stocking, 3½" × 4¾" (9 cm × 12 cm)

Materials & Supplies

For each ornament:

◆ Scraps of fancy fabrics (moirés, satins, and silks)
◆ 8" (20 cm) square fancy fabric (moiré or satin)
◆ Two 7" (18 cm) squares muslin
◆ 6" × 14" (15 cm × 36 cm) square Pellon Fleece
◆ Embroidery floss or silk buttonhole twist
◆ Ribbons
◆ Beads, Nymo thread, and #10 sharps needle
◆ Buttons
◆ Lace, ruffled or plain, for embellishing and edging
◆ ½ yard (0.46 m) rattail
◆ Hanging cord*
◆ 10" (25 cm) square art board
◆ 6" (15 cm) square milky template plastic
◆ Large darning needle and heavy thread
◆ Aleene's Original Tacky Glue
◆ Water-erasable pen

*Make from 6" (15 cm) pieces of rattail. Twist two or three different colors together and tie each end with a twist knot, leaving ½" (12 mm) tails.

Instructions

1. Using fancy fabric scraps, work crazy quilting on one muslin square. Start with a small piece of dark fabric in the center. The piece should have at least five angles. Working clockwise (counterclockwise if left-handed), sew down five fat fabric rectangles in turn. After all five pieces are sewn down, cut them into smaller, irregular shapes and begin the next round. Work until the muslin is covered. Press.
2. Choose the ornament you want to make. Trace the actual-size pattern outline onto template plastic. Cut out to form a window template.
3. Using the window template as a pattern, trace two shapes on art board, three on fleece, and one on remaining muslin. Cut out and put aside.

4. Lay the template over the crazy quilt piece. Twist and turn the window template until you see a pleasing design. Trace around the edges with a water-erasable pen.
5. Cut out ½" (12 mm) beyond the marked line. (The extra allowance will be wrapped around the art board and fleece.)
6. Begin embellishing! Glue ribbons and laces in place. Press with a warm iron. Now add the Victorian stitches. Be sure thread is a bright contrasting color. You want the stitches to show!
7. Add beads to highlight the stitches.
8. Add buttons, using embroidery floss.

Assembly:

1. Place fancy fabric on a flat surface, wrong side up. Smooth glue on one side of the art board shape. Place shape, glue side down, on the fancy fabric. Trim fabric ½" (12 mm) from art board edge.
2. Clip the fabric every ½" (12 mm) or so. Lay a bead of glue along the edge of the art board and fold the clipped edges over. Finger-press as you go. Make sure the edges are smooth. Set aside.

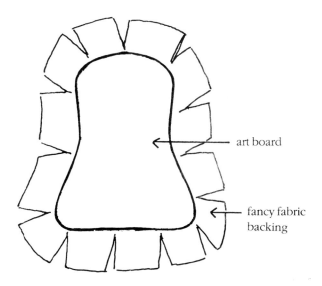

art board

fancy fabric backing

3. Starting from the bottom, stack the muslin, art board, three pieces of fleece, and the crazy quilt piece. The crazy quilt piece will be a bit larger. Turn stack over.

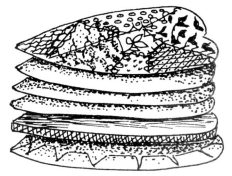

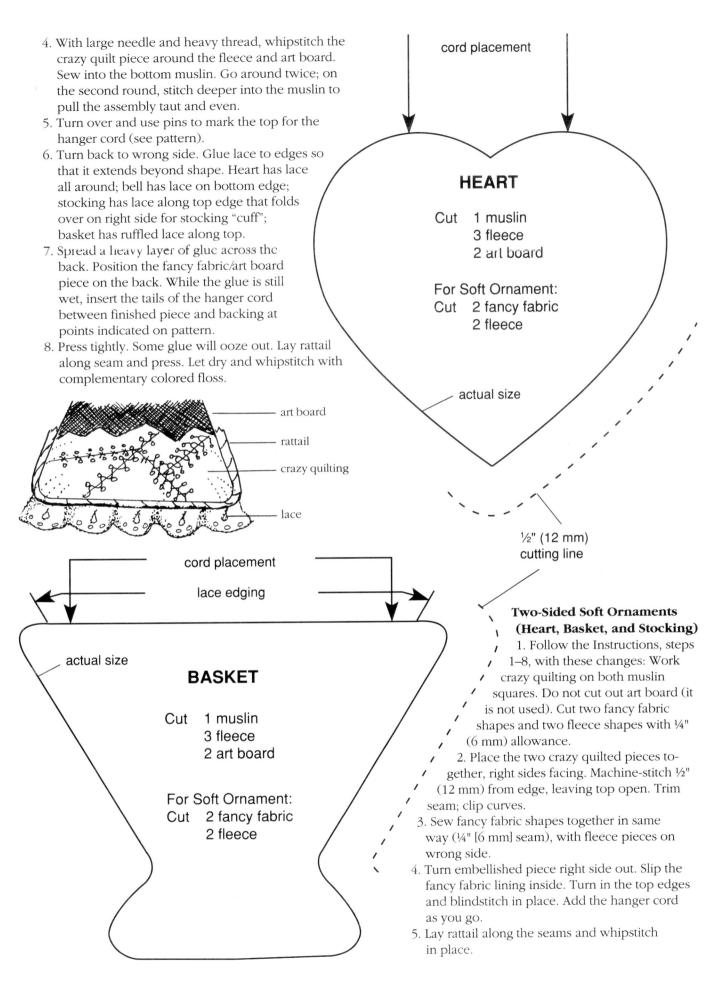

4. With large needle and heavy thread, whipstitch the crazy quilt piece around the fleece and art board. Sew into the bottom muslin. Go around twice; on the second round, stitch deeper into the muslin to pull the assembly taut and even.

5. Turn over and use pins to mark the top for the hanger cord (see pattern).

6. Turn back to wrong side. Glue lace to edges so that it extends beyond shape. Heart has lace all around; bell has lace on bottom edge; stocking has lace along top edge that folds over on right side for stocking "cuff"; basket has ruffled lace along top.

7. Spread a heavy layer of glue across the back. Position the fancy fabric/art board piece on the back. While the glue is still wet, insert the tails of the hanger cord between finished piece and backing at points indicated on pattern.

8. Press tightly. Some glue will ooze out. Lay rattail along seam and press. Let dry and whipstitch with complementary colored floss.

art board
rattail
crazy quilting
lace

cord placement

HEART

Cut   1 muslin
        3 fleece
        2 art board

For Soft Ornament:
Cut   2 fancy fabric
        2 fleece

actual size

½" (12 mm)
cutting line

cord placement

lace edging

actual size

BASKET

Cut   1 muslin
        3 fleece
        2 art board

For Soft Ornament:
Cut   2 fancy fabric
        2 fleece

Two-Sided Soft Ornaments (Heart, Basket, and Stocking)

1. Follow the Instructions, steps 1–8, with these changes: Work crazy quilting on both muslin squares. Do not cut out art board (it is not used). Cut two fancy fabric shapes and two fleece shapes with ¼" (6 mm) allowance.

2. Place the two crazy quilted pieces together, right sides facing. Machine-stitch ½" (12 mm) from edge, leaving top open. Trim seam; clip curves.

3. Sew fancy fabric shapes together in same way (¼" [6 mm] seam), with fleece pieces on wrong side.

4. Turn embellished piece right side out. Slip the fancy fabric lining inside. Turn in the top edges and blindstitch in place. Add the hanger cord as you go.

5. Lay rattail along the seams and whipstitch in place.

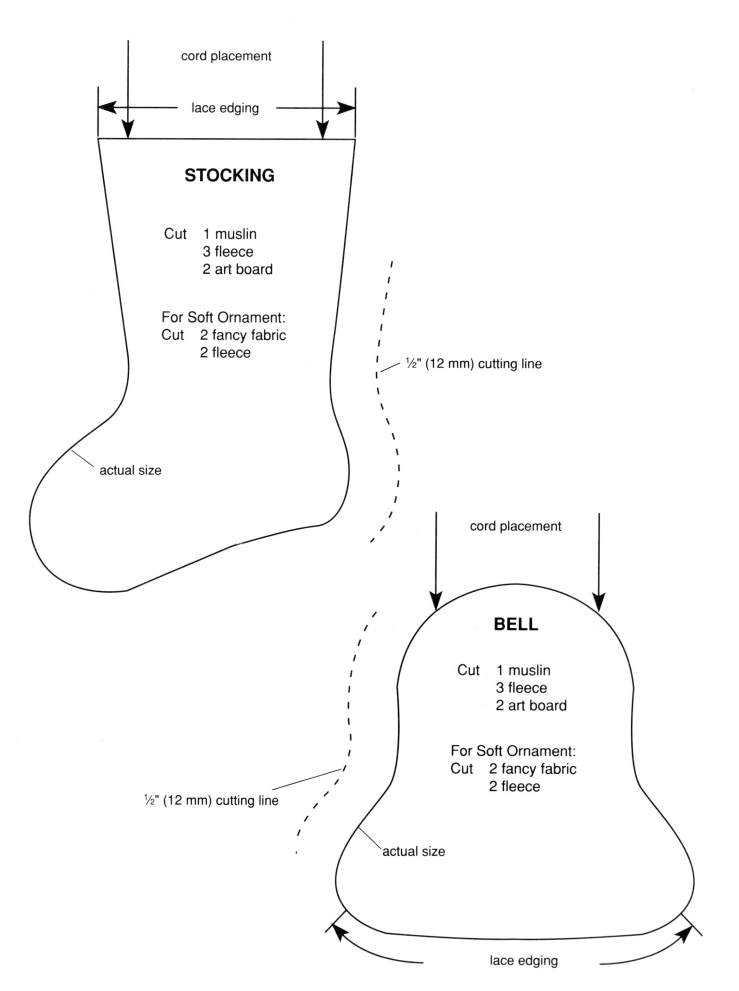

cord placement

lace edging

STOCKING

Cut 1 muslin
3 fleece
2 art board

For Soft Ornament:
Cut 2 fancy fabric
2 fleece

½" (12 mm) cutting line

actual size

cord placement

BELL

Cut 1 muslin
3 fleece
2 art board

For Soft Ornament:
Cut 2 fancy fabric
2 fleece

½" (12 mm) cutting line

actual size

lace edging

PUNCH NEEDLE ROOSTER PURSE

A very handsome fellow indeed! I used this rooster on a purse, but he'd also make a wonderful pillow or an insert for a garment. Use a firm, tightly woven fabric such as moiré, linen, cotton velveteen, or cotton. Complete the punch needle first and then cut out the oval for purse. *Photo P-9*

Size: 7" × 9" (18 cm × 23 cm) oval

Materials & Supplies

◆ ⅓ yard (0.35 m) 44"–45" fancy fabric for front, back, and lining

◆ 12" × 27" (30 cm × 69 cm) iron-on interfacing

◆ 9" × 22" (23 cm × 56 cm) Pellon Fleece

◆ Embroidery floss—gold, dark brown, dark red, medium red, light red, royal blue, light blue, teal green, wine, purple, medium brown, rusty orange, black, dark rust

◆ Black bead for eye

◆ Twisted cord*

◆ Decorative buttons for finishing cord attachments

◆ 10" × 12" (25 cm × 30 cm) milky template plastic

◆ Single-strand and medium punch needles (Igolochkoy™, #1 and #3; O Sew Easy, original Russian needle and the silver needle; see Source Guide)

◆ Susan Bates® Deluxe Embroidery Hoop & Frame, 7" (18 cm) diameter

OR

◆ Wrapped wooden hoop (must hold fabric drum-tight)

◆ Aleene's Original Tacky Glue

*Make from four or more cords cut three times the desired length; for 50" (127 cm) twisted cord, cut 150" (381 cm). See page 78 for instructions.

Instructions

1. From fancy fabric, cut a rectangle about 10" × 12" (25 cm × 30 cm). Using a light box, trace rooster (page 108) on the wrong side. Do not cut out.

2. Place fabric in hoop. Following the diagram, punch with embroidery floss from the back. Add bead eye to the front.

3. Press into terry towel from the back.

4. Trace oval on template plastic and cut out for pattern (includes ¼" (6 mm) seam allowance).

5. Fuse iron-on interfacing to back of punch needle piece and back of fancy fabric. Place pattern on right side of punched fabric, centering rooster inside oval. Trace around pattern and cut out. From fancy fabric, use pattern to cut one purse back and two linings. Cut two fleece.

6. Assemble as for Half-Circle Purse, steps 4–5 (page 97), making ¼" (6 mm) seam allowance. Whip-stitch halves together; leave top open between dots. Create your own cord trim and strap.

PUNCH NEEDLE FLORAL

This is a little exercise in using the three different sizes of punch needle—the traditional needle, which uses one strand of floss or metallic; the medium needle, which uses the equivalent of three strands (can be a mix); and the largest, which is used for silk or polyester ribbon. Color choice is up to you. Relax and have fun! Use your finished piece as a picture or box insert, or work it into a garment, purse, or pillow. *Photo P-8*

Size: Design area, 5¾" × 6¼" (15 cm × 16 cm)

Materials & Supplies

◆ 12" (30 cm) square firm, tightly woven fabric such as linen.

◆ 4 mm silk ribbon in a variety of floral colors—teal, purple, pink, fuchsia, peach, pale green

◆ Embroidery floss—dark green, medium green, fuchsia, brown, and rust

◆ Beads, Nymo thread, and #10 sharps needle

◆ Small buttons

◆ Single-strand, medium, and large punch needles (Igolochkoy, #1, #3, and #6; O Sew Easy, original Russian needle, silver needle, and blue needle)

◆ Susan Bates Deluxe Embroidery Hoop & Frame, 7" (18 cm) diameter

OR

◆ Wrapped wooden hoop (must hold fabric drum-tight)

Instructions

1. Trace floral pattern (page 109) onto wrong side of linen.

2. Place linen in hoop. Following stitch guide, punch design from back.

3. On right side, add beads to highlight the flowers.

4. Add buttons as extra flowers.

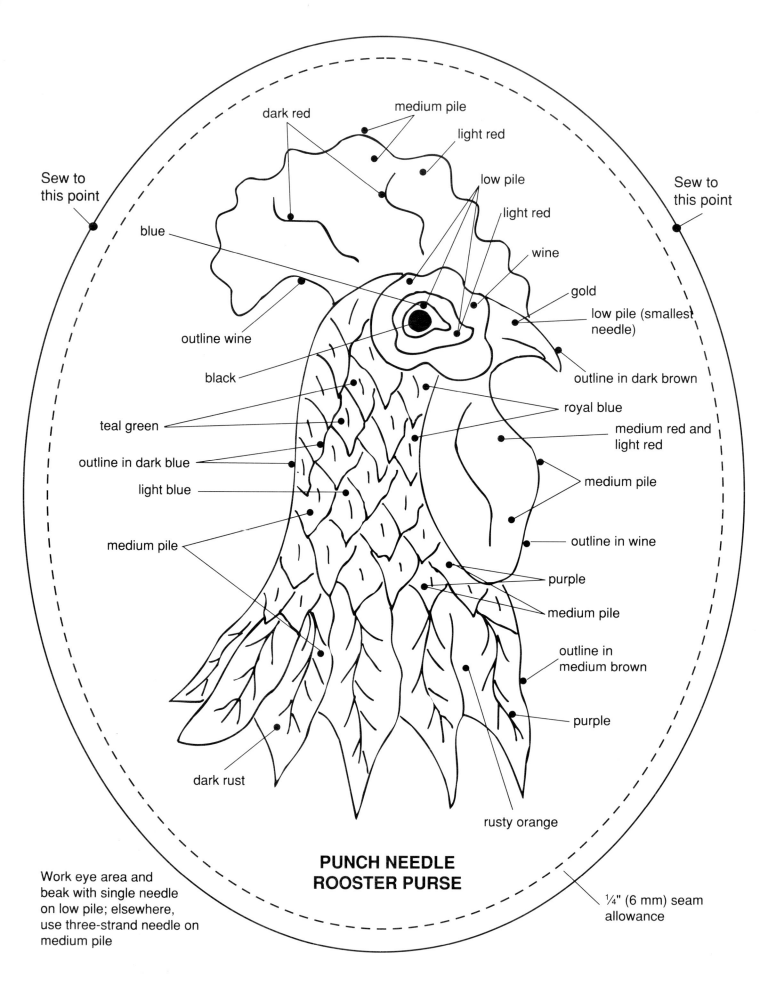

dark red

medium pile

light red

low pile

light red

wine

gold

Sew to this point

Sew to this point

blue

low pile (smallest needle)

outline wine

outline in dark brown

black

royal blue

teal green

medium red and light red

outline in dark blue

medium pile

light blue

outline in wine

medium pile

purple

medium pile

outline in medium brown

dark rust

purple

rusty orange

PUNCH NEEDLE ROOSTER PURSE

Work eye area and beak with single needle on low pile; elsewhere, use three-strand needle on medium pile

¼" (6 mm) seam allowance

PUNCH NEEDLE FLORAL

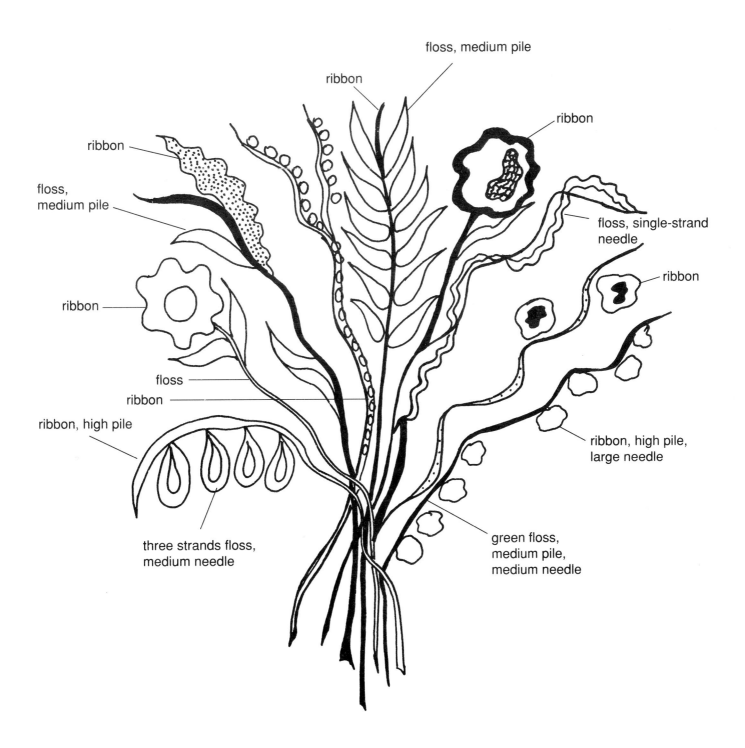

floss, medium pile

ribbon

ribbon

ribbon

floss,
medium pile

floss, single-strand
needle

ribbon

ribbon

floss

ribbon

ribbon, high pile

ribbon, high pile,
large needle

three strands floss,
medium needle

green floss,
medium pile,
medium needle

RIBBON EMBROIDERY BROOCHES

A very simple pattern for the beginner, in two sizes. These brooches are lovely and feminine—you'll want to make dozens for gifts and various outfits. *Photo P-6*

Sizes: Ovals 1½" × 2½" (4 cm x 6 cm) and 1⅞" × 2½" (5 cm × 6 cm)

Materials & Supplies

- 6" (15 cm) square firm, tightly woven fabric such as linen, silk, moiré, and synthetics.
- 3" (8 cm) square muslin
- 3" (8 cm) square leather for backing
- 3" × 9" (8 cm × 23 cm) strip Pellon Fleece
- 4 mm silk ribbon in a variety of floral colors— pink, fuchsia, purple, green
- Embroidery floss or silk buttonhole twist in green and gold
- Beads, Nymo thread, #10 sharps needle
- 8" (20 cm) fancy cord
- 1" (2.5 cm) jeweler's brooch pin
- 3" (8 cm) square art board
- 4" × 6" (10 cm × 15 cm) milky template plastic
- 3" (8 cm) hoop
- Large darning needle and heavy thread.
- Aleene's Original Tacky Glue
- Water-erasable pen

Instructions

Remember that ribbon embroidery patterns are suggested by circles, lines, dots, and other symbols. Use your imagination for filling in.

1. Lay the fabric square over the pattern, right side up, and draw in lines. If the fabric is too dark for tracing, use a transfer pencil or "free-form" it. Do not cut out oval.
2. Place fabric in hoop. Following Stitch Key, embroider ribbon flowers and leaves.
3. Add extra embroidery with floss or silk buttonhole twist. Highlight with beads.
4. Trace oval (solid line) on template plastic and cut out for pattern. Mark oval with water-erasable pen on ribbon embroidery, and cut out ½" (12 mm) beyond marked line. (This allowance is turned to the back; see pattern.)
5. Cut one muslin, one leather, one art board, and two fleece ovals. Mark a third fleece oval and cut out ¼" (6 mm) beyond marked line.
6. Assemble as for barrette, steps 1–4 (page 98), wrapping with fancy cord. Glue jeweler's pin to back.

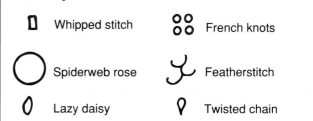

Stitch Key	
🄳 Whipped stitch	⠿ French knots
◯ Spiderweb rose	Featherstitch
◗ Lazy daisy	Twisted chain

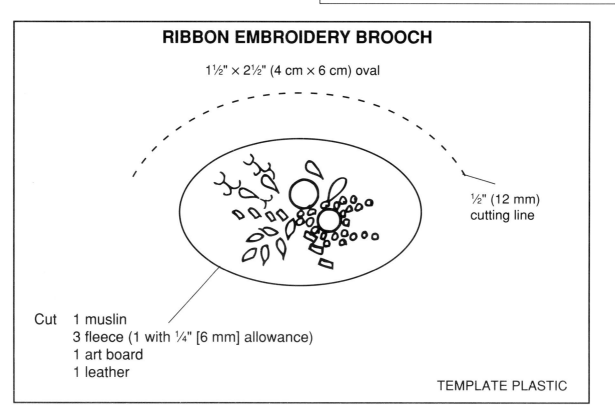

RIBBON EMBROIDERY BROOCH

1½" × 2½" (4 cm × 6 cm) oval

½" (12 mm) cutting line

Cut   1 muslin
        3 fleece (1 with ¼" [6 mm] allowance)
        1 art board
        1 leather

TEMPLATE PLASTIC

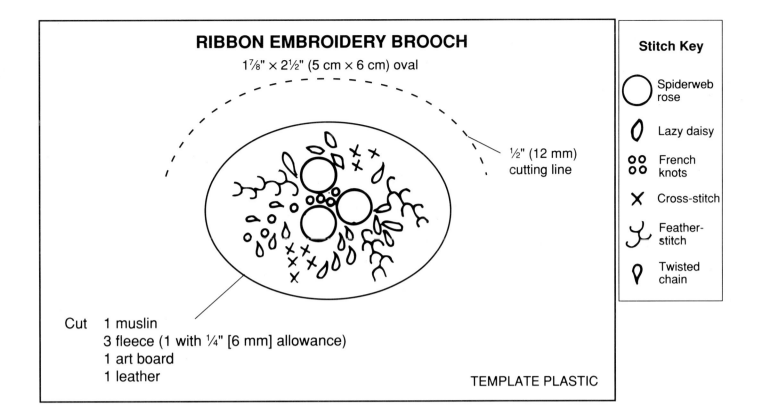

RIBBON EMBROIDERY BROOCH

1⅞" × 2½" (5 cm × 6 cm) oval

½" (12 mm)
cutting line

Cut   1 muslin
        3 fleece (1 with ¼" [6 mm] allowance)
        1 art board
        1 leather

TEMPLATE PLASTIC

Stitch Key

◯ Spiderweb rose

◊ Lazy daisy

○○
○○ French knots

✕ Cross-stitch

Feather-stitch

Twisted chain

RIBBON EMBROIDERY FLORAL PENDANT

A confection of clear, vibrant colors is topped off with ribbon roses and embroidery! Fine cords are tightly braided, then allowed to release into a tassel. *Photo P-6*

Size: 4½" (11 cm) diameter.

Materials & Supplies

- Scraps of solid color fabrics, at least six pieces
- 6" (15 cm) square leather for backing
- Two 6" (15 cm) squares muslin
- 15" (38 cm) square Pellon fleece
- Embroidery floss
- Two 12" (30 cm) lengths ½" (12 mm) satin ribbon in different colors
- One 12" (30 cm) length ¼" (6 mm) satin ribbon
- A variety of 4 mm silk ribbons, including two shades of green
- Green 1" (2.5 cm) satin ribbon for leaves
- Beads, Nymo thread, and #10 sharps needle
- 4" (10 cm) hoop
- Pearl buttons, small and dainty
- Assorted fine cords, at least 2¾ yards (2.5 m) each
- Large beads and some doodads
- 6" (15 cm) square art board
- 8" (20 cm) square milky template plastic
- Large darning needle and heavy thread
- Aleene's Original Tacky Glue
- Water-erasable pen

Instructions

1. Place template plastic on circle pattern (page 112) and trace. Cut out for window template.
2. Using window template as a pattern, cut one muslin, three fleece, one art board, and one leather.
3. Place small piece of dark fabric in the center of the remaining muslin square. The piece should have at least five angles. Working clockwise (counter-clockwise if left-handed), sew down five fat fabric rectangles in turn. After all five pieces are sewn down, cut them into smaller, irregular shapes and begin the next round. Work until the muslin is covered. Press.
4. Place the window template on the crazy quilting and move it around until you find a design placement that you like. Mark with water-erasable pen.
5. Embroider each seam with Victorian stitches. Do not stitch beyond the marked line.
6. Using the water-erasable pen, mark circles for the ribbon flowers.
7. With 12" (30 cm) satin ribbons, make three concertina roses and sew in place.

8. Place the foundation piece in the hoop and work the ribbon embroidery. Make ribbon leaves (page 75) and tack in place.

9. Add beads and miniature buttons; embellish buttons with beads.

10. Using floss or 4 mm silk ribbon, embroider twigs, leaves, and stems.

11. Remove from hoop and cut ½" (12 mm) beyond marked circle.

12. Make an 18" (46 cm) twisted cord (page 78) to circle the pendant and form a tassel. Braid the remaining cord tightly (use a variety of cords for added interest). Adjust to neck length and knot at both ends. Assemble as for oval pendant, steps 1–5 (page 98).

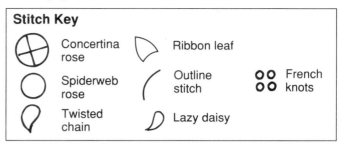

Stitch Key

⊕ Concertina rose	◣ Ribbon leaf	
○ Spiderweb rose	⌒ Outline stitch	ᐤᐤ ᐤᐤ French knots
◗ Twisted chain	⟆ Lazy daisy	

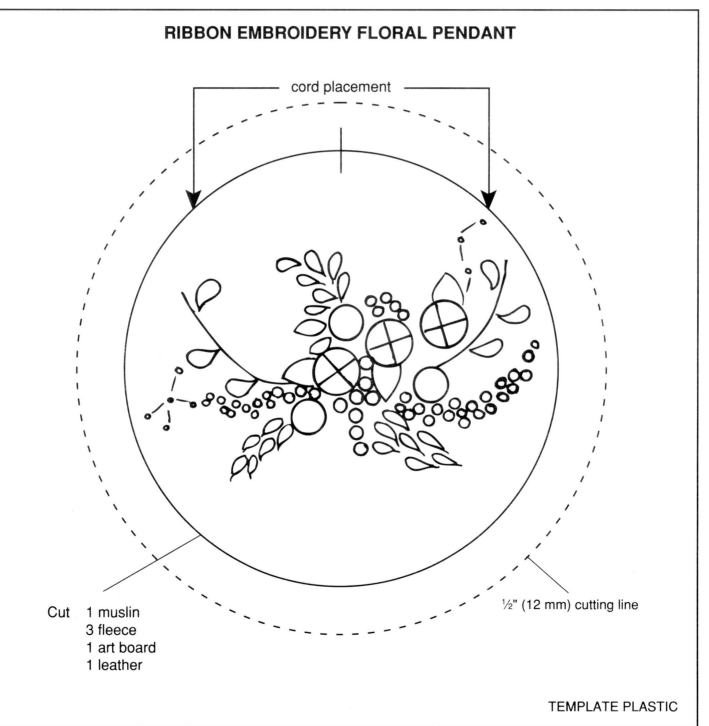

RIBBON EMBROIDERY FLORAL PENDANT

cord placement

½" (12 mm) cutting line

Cut   1 muslin
        3 fleece
        1 art board
        1 leather

TEMPLATE PLASTIC

BUTTON-JEWELED BELT

This elegant hip belt can be worn low on the hips and off to the side, or higher and centered. It is adapted from an out-of-print Vogue pattern.* It is a piece of jewelry unto itself—a wonderful way to show off a special button collection. *Photo P-13*

Size: About 45" (114 cm) long; adjust to fit during assembly.

Materials & Supplies

◆ Variety of fancy fabric scraps (at least a dozen)

◆ Small piece Ultrasuede fabric or leather (for slip loop)

◆ ⅓ yard (0.30 m) 44"–45" lining fabric

◆ ⅓ yard (0.30 m) 44"–45" muslin

◆ ½ yard (0.46 m) 44"–45" extra-heavy iron-on interfacing

◆ Sturdy lace (to withstand heavy wear)

◆ Ribbons

◆ Embroidery floss or silk buttonhole twist (a variety)

◆ Beads, Nymo thread, and #10 sharps needle

◆ Buttons

◆ 10" (25 cm) strip Velcro fastener

◆ Spray starch

Instructions

1. Trace and cut out pattern pieces A, B, C, and D.
2. From Ultrasuede fabric or leather, cut one slip loop D. Fold lengthwise, right side in. With a ¼" seam allowance, machine-stitch along long edge. Turn out and set aside.
3. From lining fabric, cut one A, two B, and two C. From iron-on interfacing, cut three A, six B, and six C.

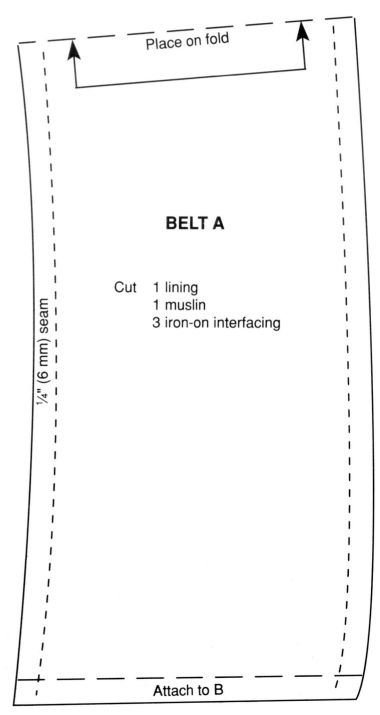

Place on fold

BELT A

Cut   1 lining
      1 muslin
      3 iron-on interfacing

¼" (6 mm) seam

Attach to B

*Courtesy Butterick Company, Inc.

4. Fuse a double layer of iron-on interfacing to each lining piece. Sew A, B, and C lining pieces together and set aside. Sew remaining A, B, and C iron-on interfacing pieces together and set aside.

5. From muslin, cut one A, two B, and two C, adding ½" (12 mm) allowance all around. Sew each B to a C, making ¾" (18 mm) seam; trim seam to ¼" (6 mm).

6. Using fancy fabric scraps, work crazy quilting on the three muslin units. Fill each unit separately to prevent the work from looking strippy. Join the muslin units with ¾" seams to take up extra allowance.(To hide the seams, peel back crazy quilting, sew muslin, then overlap and appliqué crazy quilting; see page 46).

7. Spray-starch the wrong side for extra body and press. Fuse the iron-on interfacing to the wrong side. Cut on the pattern line.

8. Lay down laces and ribbons (make sure they run edge to edge). Tack firmly into place.

9. Cover remaining seams with Victorian stitches.

10. Add bead and button embellishments. Before finishing, drape the belt around your hips and mark the position for the slip loop. Sew it into place. Sew buttons to the loop using extra heavy thread. Anchor with a button at each end.

11. Place belt and lining right sides together. With a ¼" (6 mm) seam allowance, machine-stitch all around, leaving an opening at one end. Carefully turn out. Place crazy quilting face down into a terry towel and press.

12. Try on belt. Mark position for hidden Velcro strip to hold end in place. Glue on Velcro, then secure with hand stitching.

Attach to A

BELT B

Cut 2 lining
2 muslin (add ½" [12 mm] allowance all around)
6 iron-on interfacing

¼" (6 mm) seam

Lengthen or shorten here

Attach to C

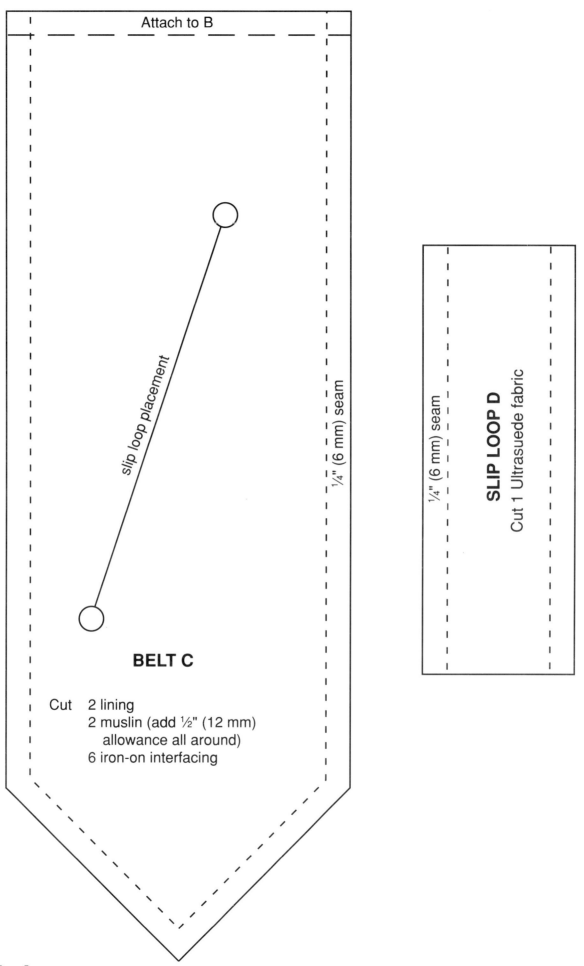

Attach to B

slip loop placement

¼" (6 mm) seam

BELT C

Cut 2 lining
2 muslin (add ½" (12 mm)
   allowance all around)
6 iron-on interfacing

¼" (6 mm) seam

SLIP LOOP D
Cut 1 Ultrasuede fabric

CRYSTAL POUCH

This pattern is for my daughter Madeleine and all those who collect crystals and unusual stones. It is just big enough to hold about five pieces. It can also be used as a key pouch. *Photo P-5*

Size: 3" × 4½" (8 cm × 11 cm)

Materials & Supplies

- ◆ Four or five Ultrasuede fabric scraps in various colors
- ◆ 9" × 16" (23 cm × 41 cm) Ultrasuede fabric
- ◆ Embroidery threads
- ◆ Beads, Nymo thread, and #10 sharps or beading needle
- ◆ Doodads and buttons
- ◆ Two cords of equal length for hanging strap
- ◆ Assorted tassels
- ◆ Velcro fastener

OR

- ◆ Large snap closure
- ◆ Aleene's Original Tacky Glue
- ◆ Candle and matches
- ◆ Tweezers
- ◆ Awl
- ◆ Pinking sheers

Instructions

1. Trace patterns, including ⅛" (3 mm) seam allowance. From Ultrasuede, cut one pouch and two sides.
2. On pouch, decide an angle for the overlap and lightly draw a guideline. Cut out ¼" (6 mm) beyond the line. Light the candle and singe the edges down to the line. Be sure to work in a ventilated area as this step is very smelly.
3. Decide on pleasing patterns for the scraps or follow the color photograph. Burn the edges, using a tweezer to hold the pieces close to the flame. Use tiny dots of glue to set in place on the flap. Set sewing machine at a long stitch and sew down with matching thread.
4. Assemble pouch: Sew two side pieces to pouch with seams facing out! Begin sewing from the unburned edge, allowing the burned section to fall over the front as a flap. Trim seams with pinking shears.
5. Embellish with beads and doodads. Be careful not to sew through to the back of the flap. Hide the stitches in the layers.
6. Using awl, punch four holes at top of each side piece (a). Punch the outside holes through two layers. Decide how you want to wear the pouch—as a swing purse, necklace, or looped over a

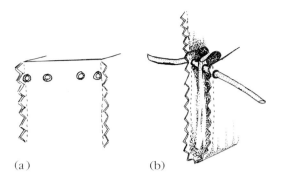

(a)   (b)

belt—and choose the appropriate lengths for the cords.

They can be single, braided, or twisted cords.

7. Thread the two separate cord units through the four holes on each side. Gather the cords at the top and tie a knot to form a tassle. Decorate the tassel and add other tassels if desired.
8. Add beads along the outer seam lines if you wish.
9. Add Velcro or snap closure underneath flap.

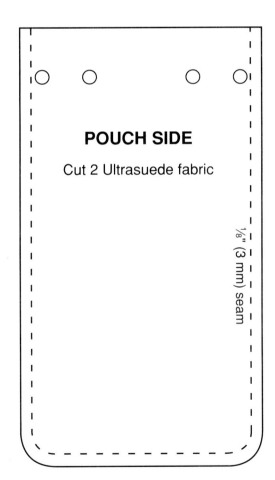

POUCH SIDE

Cut 2 Ultrasuede fabric

⅛" (3 mm) seam

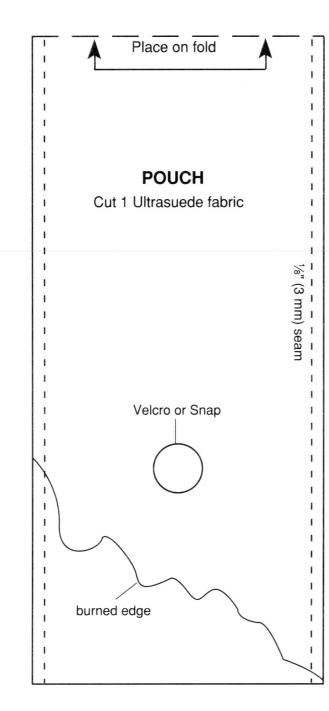

Place on fold

POUCH

Cut 1 Ultrasuede fabric

⅛" (3 mm) seam

Velcro or Snap

burned edge

- 13" (33 cm) square Pellon Fleece
- Embroidery threads
- Beads, Nymo thread, and #10 sharps needle
- Medium size punch needle (optional)
- Small embroidery hoop (optional)
- Candle and matches
- Aleene's Original Tacky Glue
- Masking tape
- Water-erasable pen
- Picture frame with 5" × 7" (13 cm × 18 cm) opening

Instructions

1. Using water-erasable pen, trace pattern (page 118), including ½" (12 mm) seam allowance, onto muslin.
2. Lay down the sky fabric (1).
3. Transfer the mountain shapes 2, 3, 4, and 5 to the silky fabrics you've chosen. Cut out ¼" (6 mm) beyond trace lines. Light the candle and place in a safe, well-ventilated area. Burn the "mountain" edges down to the trace lines.
4. Lay mountains in position. With a toothpick, dot on tacky fabric glue to hold them in place temporarily until you can embroider them down. As you work, use the picture frame as a window template, laying it down on your work to check the placement.
5. Cut out the horizontal holding piece 6 and sew in, anchoring the mountains. Lay in foreground pieces 7 and 8.
6. Press and spray-starch on the wrong side.
7. Cut out piece ½" (12 mm) beyond the inner frame line (the allowance is glued into the frame).
8. Embroider with a variety of stitches. Use small stitches within the mountain shapes. Embellish with beads.
9. To add punch needle, hold the fabric taut, wrong side up, in a small hoop. Use the seam and embroidery line as guides for punching in ground cover. Hold the piece up to a window or over a light box to draw trees in position on the wrong side.
10. Using the frame as a template, cut two fleece pieces to exactly the same measurement as the opening and a third piece ¼" (6 mm) larger all around.
11. Turn the frame wrong side up and lay beads of glue along the rabbet groove. Lay the finished piece face down and tape it into place. Let the glue dry.
12. Lay the larger fleece down on the picture back, then the two remaining fleece. Glue on backing, wedging fleece in between.

LANDSCAPE SCENE

Here is a Southwest scene that you may enjoy working for practice. Use my pattern pieces just to get the feel of it. You can adjust the sky area or foreground to fit a larger dimension (cut the muslin base in a larger size). *Photo P-10*

Size: 5" × 7" (13 cm × 18 cm)

Materials & Supplies

- Sky blue fabric (any type but velvet)
- Silk or silky fabrics for the mountains
- A variety of fabrics for the foreground. Keep the patterns muted.
- 12" (30 cm) square muslin

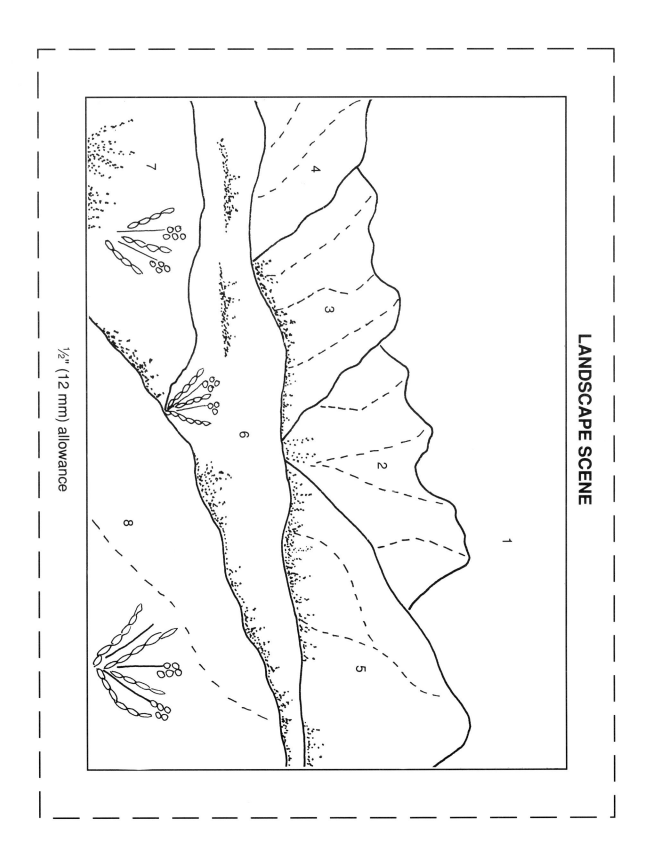

½" (12 mm) allowance

LANDSCAPE SCENE

WEEPING HEART PENDANT

A large heart pendant that gives you lots of room for embellishments. The weeping heart can be traditional or contemporary. *Photo P-11*

Size: 3¼" × 3¾" (8 cm × 10 cm)

Materials & Supplies

- ◆ Five to eight scraps of fancy fabrics, including solids, prints, and textures. Be sure to include a dark solid (for center).
- ◆ 5" (13 cm) square leather
- ◆ Two 6" (15 cm) squares muslin
- ◆ 5" × 15" (13 cm × 38 cm) Pellon Fleece
- ◆ Ribbons for embroidery (optional)
- ◆ Embroidery floss or silk buttonhole twist
- ◆ Beads, Nymo thread, and #10 sharps needle
- ◆ Buttons and doodads
- ◆ 1¼ yards (1.15 m) each assorted cords for neck cord
- ◆ 12" (0.30 m) rattail or other trim for edging
- ◆ Tassel (optional)
- ◆ Aluminum Indian dance cones (optional)
- ◆ 6" (15 cm) square heavy art board
- ◆ 9" (23 cm) square milky template plastic
- ◆ Large darning needle and heavy thread
- ◆ Aleene's Original Tacky Glue
- ◆ Water-erasable pen

Instructions

1. Trace heart onto template plastic and cut out.
2. Using window template as a pattern, mark and cut out one muslin, three fleece, one art board, and one leather. Do not add seam allowances.
3. The remaining muslin square is the base for the crazy quilting. From dark solid, cut a small center piece with five angles and position on muslin. Working clockwise (counterclockwise if left-handed), sew down five fat fabric rectangles in turn. After all five pieces are sewn down, cut them into smaller, irregular shapes and begin the next round. Work until the muslin is covered. Press.
4. Lay the heart template on the crazy quilting and move it around until you find a design placement that you like. Mark with the water-erasable pen, then cut out ½" (12 mm) outside marked line. (This allowance is turned to the back; see pattern.)
5. Embroider each seam with decorative stitches. Add ribbon embroidery if desired. Embellish with French knots, beads, buttons, and doodads.
6. Starting from the bottom, stack muslin, art board, three pieces of fleece, and crazy quilt heart, which will be a bit larger than the others. Turn stack over.

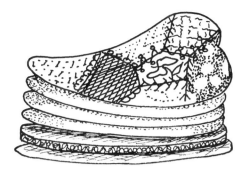

7. With large needle and heavy thread, whipstitch the crazy quilt heart around the fleece and art board. Sew into bottom muslin. Go around twice; on the second round, stitch deeper into the muslin to pull the assembly taut and even.
8. Twist neck cords together and cut to a length you like. Tie a slip knot at each end, leaving a ½" (12 mm) tail.
9. Spread a heavy layer of glue across the back and affix leather backing. While the glue is still wet, insert the tails of the neck cord between heart and backing at points indicated on pattern.

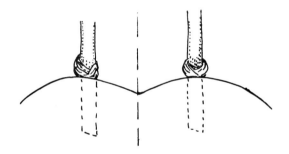

10. Press tightly. Some glue will ooze out. Starting at center top, lay rattail or trim along edge and press. For a different look, add a tassel or aluminum Indian dance cones.

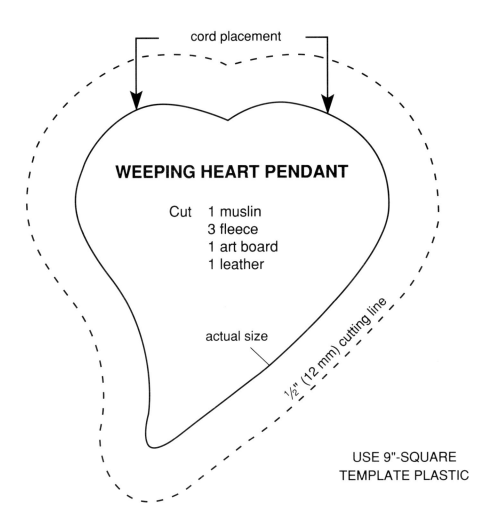

cord placement

WEEPING HEART PENDANT

Cut   1 muslin
         3 fleece
         1 art board
         1 leather

actual size

½" (12 mm) cutting line

USE 9"-SQUARE
TEMPLATE PLASTIC

VICTORIAN PICTURE FRAME

Admire the one you love in a romantic Victorian picture frame. The mood can be light and airy or dark and seductive! These frames make beautiful gifts for special occasions such as weddings, anniversaries, and christenings. This pattern is courtesy of Anne's Glory Box.
Photo P-12

Size: 7" × 9½" (18 cm × 24 cm)

Materials & Supplies
- Fancy fabrics in a variety of solids, patterns, and textures—at least 12 different pieces
- ⅓ yard (0.30 m) 44"–45" fancy fabric for backing, lining, and prop
- 12" (30 cm) square muslin
- ⅓ yard (0.30 m) 45" Pellon Fleece
- Embroidery floss or silk buttonhole twist (a variety)
- Laces
- Ribbons
- Beads, Nymo thread, and #10 sharps needle
- Decorative buttons and doodads
- 1⅓ yards (1.25 m) fancy braid
- 1 sheet (20" × 30" [51 cm × 76 cm]) medium weight art board
- 12" × 14" (30 cm × 36 cm) milky template plastic
- Aleene's Original Tacky Glue
- Water-erasable marker
- Spray starch

Instructions
1. Trace the prop and frame patterns (pages 121 and 122) onto template plastic and cut out for patterns.
2. On fancy fabrics, mark two backs (without oval opening) and two props and cut out ½" (12 mm) beyond marked lines. On fleece, mark three fronts (with oval opening); cut out two on marked lines

and the third ¼" (6 mm) beyond marked lines. From art board, cut one front, two backs, and two props.

3. On muslin, trace frame front, including oval.
4. Cut out muslin frame front 1" (2.5 cm) beyond marked line. Do not cut out oval.
5. With fancy fabric pieces, fill in muslin frame with crazy quilting. Be aware that the oval will be cut away later. Press finished piece thoroughly on the wrong side.
6. Spray-starch the wrong side for extra body and press again.
7. Lay the template pattern down on the foundation piece and mark with water-erasable pen. Cut out ½" (12 mm) beyond marked lines. (This allowance is turned to the back; see pattern.)
8. Lay down laces and ribbon. Tack firmly into place. Fill in remaining seams with Victorian stitches.
9. Add beads and further embellishments.

Assembly:
1. Glue the three fleece pieces to the front of the art board frame, placing largest fleece on top.
2. Glue the crazy quilt frame to the padded art board front. Clip along inside and outside edges. Fold edges to back and glue.

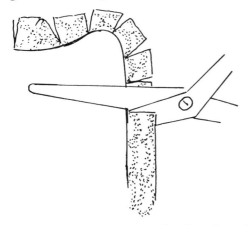

3. Spread glue across one side of each art board back. Lay fancy fabric backs, wrong side down, onto glued areas. Clip the edges; fold to back and glue.
4. Glue the two backs firmly together. Keep pressed until dry.
5. Score each art board prop on dash line. Cover with fancy fabric on unscored sides as for backs. When gluing together, leave 1" (2.5 cm) ends above scoring glue-free. Press tightly until dry.

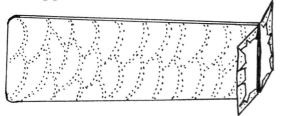

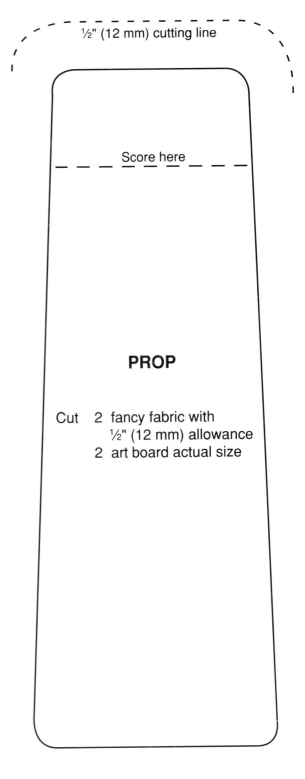

½" (12 mm) cutting line

Score here

PROP

Cut 2 fancy fabric with
½" (12 mm) allowance
2 art board actual size

6. Glue front and back together along bottom and side edges; leave the top portion free (to insert picture). Glue prop to back.
7. Lay beads of glue along joined edges and cover with fancy braid.

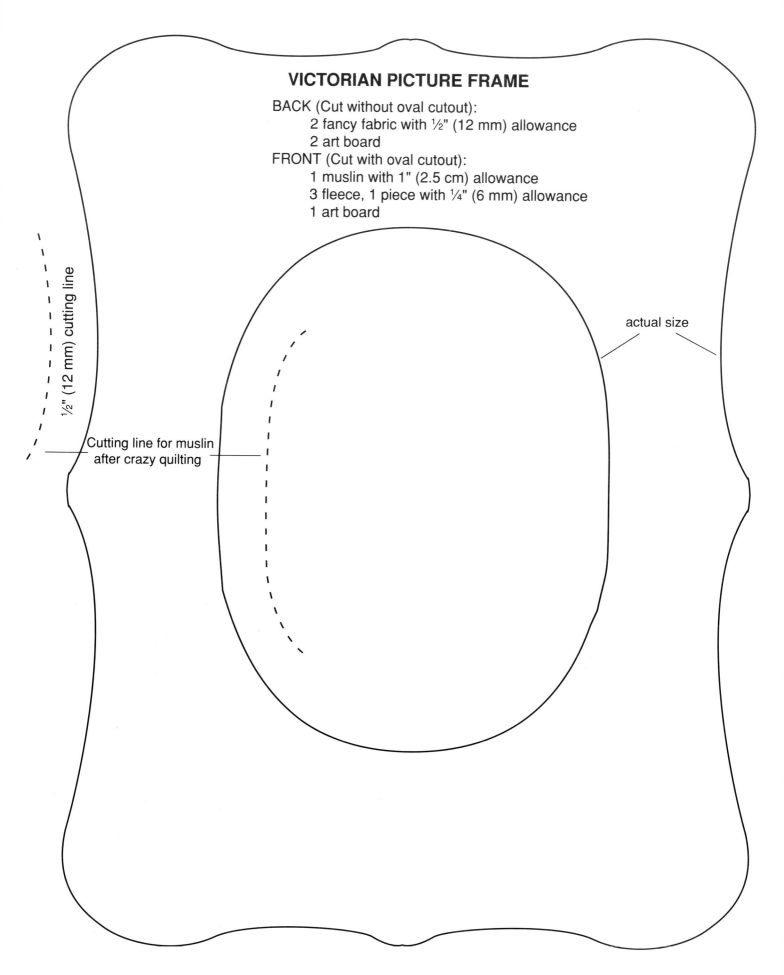

VICTORIAN PICTURE FRAME

BACK (Cut without oval cutout):
    2 fancy fabric with ½" (12 mm) allowance
    2 art board
FRONT (Cut with oval cutout):
    1 muslin with 1" (2.5 cm) allowance
    3 fleece, 1 piece with ¼" (6 mm) allowance
    1 art board

½" (12 mm) cutting line

actual size

Cutting line for muslin
after crazy quilting

Appendix

Stitch Dictionary

BULLION KNOT

Bullion knots can be used individually, side by side, or in a cluster to form a flower (see Bullion Rose). Use double thread. Bring needle up at A and go down at B, but do not pull the thread through (a). Come up again at A and bring the thread halfway through the material. Hold the needle from below and twist the thread around the needle until the twists equal the distance between A and B (c). Hold the top of the needle with finger and thumb of left hand and draw the needle through the twists (d). Use the needle to hold the twists while pulling the thread through until the knot lies flat on the material (e). Put in the needle at the end of the twist and pull through firmly.

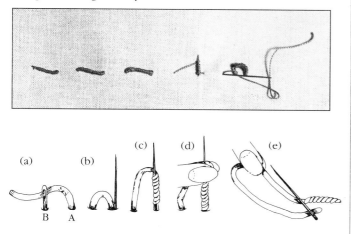

(a) (b) (c) (d) (e)

B A

BULLION ROSE

To make a rose, work three bullion knots to form a triangle (a). Then work a bullion knot to wrap around one corner of the triangle (b). Put a few extra twists on the needle so each knot curls around (c). Work around the triangle in this way until the rose is formed (d). Use shading to make the rose more realistic.

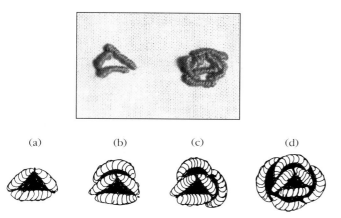

(a) (b) (c) (d)

BUTTONHOLE STITCH

This stitch is worked from left to right. Hold the thread down with your thumb and make a downward vertical stitch. Bring the needle over the thread and pull into place. The bottom line formed should lie on the seam. Make sure the vertical stitches are straight and even.

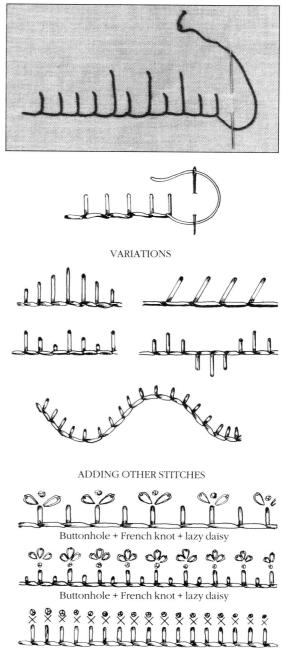

VARIATIONS

ADDING OTHER STITCHES

Buttonhole + French knot + lazy daisy

Buttonhole + French knot + lazy daisy

Buttonhole + cross-stitch + French knot

BUTTONHOLE STITCH WITH SHISHA MIRROR

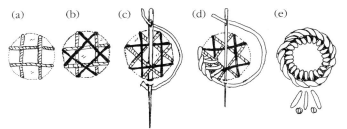

(a)   (b)   (c)   (d)   (e)

CHAINED FEATHERSTITCH

Chained featherstitch is good for decorating a ribbon. Work between two parallel lines. Bring the thread through at A and make a slanting chain stitch. Tie the stitch at B. Take a second slanting chain stitch from the right at C and tie it down at D. The tied stitches form a regular zigzag pattern.

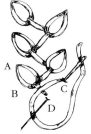

CHAIN STITCH

The chain stitch is similar to lazy daisy except that it is continuous. Pull up the thread at the starting point and hold it down with your thumb. Put the needle down into the starting point and come up again a short distance away. Be sure the needle comes up over the thread, forming a loop. Repeat to make a chain.

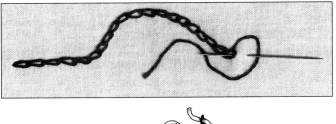

CHEVRON STITCH

Chevron stitch lies horizontally and evenly on each side of a seam. Work from left to right. Start in the lower corner and take a short stitch forward, then a half stitch back. Work alternately from one side to the other. Be sure to keep the stitches evenly spaced.

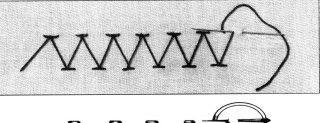

VARIATIONS

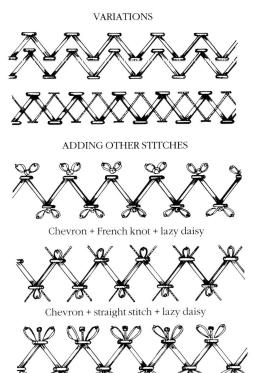

ADDING OTHER STITCHES

Chevron + French knot + lazy daisy

Chevron + straight stitch + lazy daisy

Chevron + lazy daisy + straight stitch + bead or French knot

CLOSED BUTTONHOLE STITCH

Closed buttonhole stitch is similar to buttonhole stitch, except two adjacent "vertical" stitches are worked into the same hole, forming a triangle.

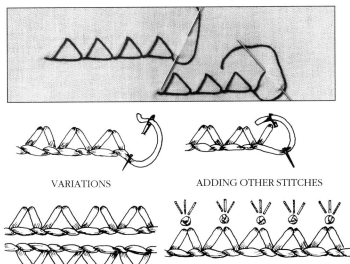

VARIATIONS   ADDING OTHER STITCHES

Closed buttonhole + French knot + fans

CORAL STITCH

Coral stitch is good for stems or fill-in work. Work horizontally, from right to left. Bring the needle up at A. Turn the needle up and down at right angles to the thread. Hold the thread under the needle and draw the needle through gently to form the knot. The length of the vertical stitch determines the size of the knot.

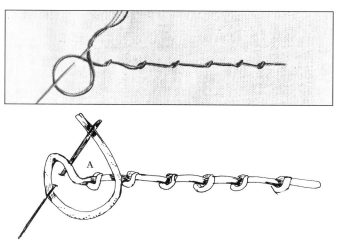

COUCHING

Couching is a decorative way to hold long threads in place. Lay down long threads as desired. Now, with either matching or contrasting thread, come up at regular intervals and wrap a small, tight stitch over the long thread.

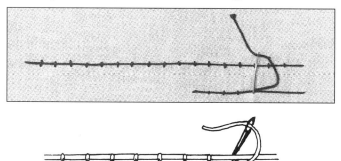

CRETAN STITCH

Cretan stitch lies evenly on both sides of a seam. Start at the lower left and work from left to right. Take short vertical stitches alternately downward and upward along each side of the seam. Hold the thread so the needle will pass over it. Be sure to keep the vertical stitches even.

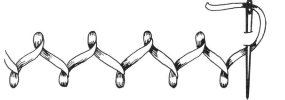

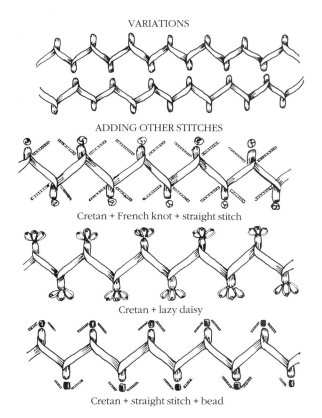

VARIATIONS

ADDING OTHER STITCHES

Cretan + French knot + straight stitch

Cretan + lazy daisy

Cretan + straight stitch + bead

CROSS-STITCH

Work cross-stitches evenly over a seam. Start at the lower right and work from right to left. First, work a row of even diagonal stitches, making each stitch from lower right to upper left. Next, work from left to right, making diagonal stitches from lower left to upper right. As each stitch overlays a stitch from the first group, it will form an **X**.

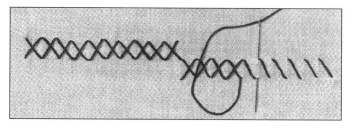

DETACHED TWISTED CHAIN

Come up at A and hold the thread with your thumb. Go down at B, even with and to the left of A. Hold the thread in a loop and bring the needle up at C, below and midway between A and B. Anchor with a long or short catch stitch.

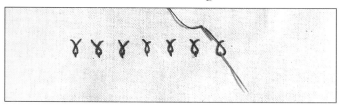

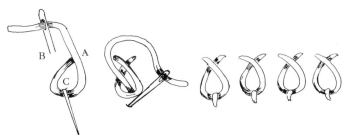

FANS

Embroidered fans are a traditional decorative touch in crazy quilting. They are very effective in a row to cover seam lines. Be sure to pull the threads firmly into place. Otherwise they will snag and lose their shape. Larger fan motifs can be highlighted with embroidery.

PHOTO DETAIL COURTESY DENVER ART MUSEUM

COMBINING STITCHES

Straight stitch +
running stitch

Straight stitch +
cross-stitch

Stem stitch + running stitch +
French knot

Straight stitch + beads + lazy daisy

Straight lines + French knots

VARIATIONS

Straight lines

Lazy daisies

Straight lines

FEATHERSTITCH

The featherstitch is a vertical stitch that you work down towards you. Begin with a single stitch and alternate back and forth. The secret is to always put the needle in at B straight across from where the thread came out at A.

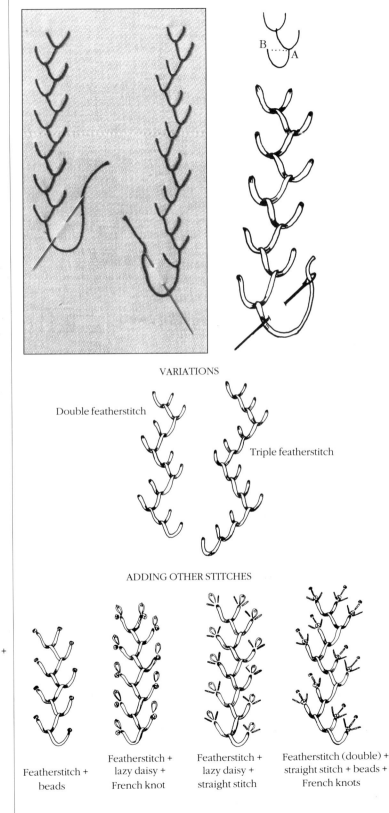

VARIATIONS

Double featherstitch

Triple featherstitch

ADDING OTHER STITCHES

Featherstitch +
beads

Featherstitch +
lazy daisy +
French knot

Featherstitch +
lazy daisy +
straight stitch

Featherstitch (double) +
straight stitch + beads +
French knots

FLY STITCH

Fly stitches may be scattered or grouped vertically. Come up at A and go down at B. Hold the thread in a loop and bring the needle up at C, below and midway between A and B. Loop the thread under the needle and draw through gently. Anchor with a long or short catch stitch. For the vertical chain, just continue down.

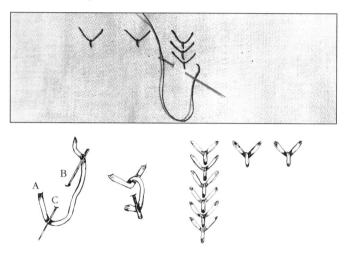

FRENCH KNOT

This stitch is just what it sounds like—a knot. Bring the needle up and circle the needle twice around the thread. Hold the thread taut as you insert the needle back into the fabric, as close as possible to the starting point. Hold the knot in place until the needle has passed through it. Secure the knot in back.

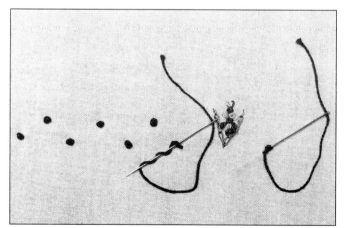

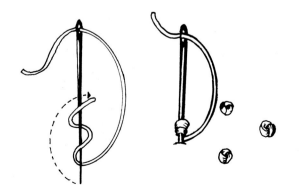

HERRINGBONE STITCH

The herringbone stitch is worked from left to right and lies evenly on both sides of the seam. Take a small horizontal backstitch on one side of the seam, then advance slightly and do the same on the opposite side. Be sure to keep the horizontal stitches even as this creates the crossing diagonal design.

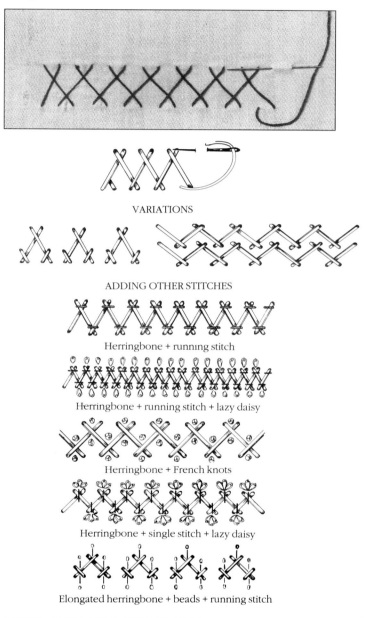

VARIATIONS

ADDING OTHER STITCHES

Herringbone + running stitch

Herringbone + running stitch + lazy daisy

Herringbone + French knots

Herringbone + single stitch + lazy daisy

Elongated herringbone + beads + running stitch

INTERLACED RUNNING STITCH

With a heavy thread, make a row of running stitches. Thread a blunt needle with a different color and weave it through the running stitch. Thread back in the other direction to make ovals of equal size. Keep the tension even.

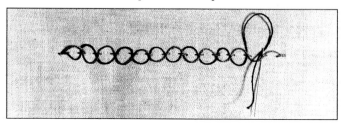

LAZY DAISY

Lazy daisy is a loop stitch—it's like a free-floating chain stitch. Bring the needle up from the back and hold the thread down with your thumb. Insert the needle at the starting point, so the thread forms a loop. Bring the needle out a short distance away—make sure the needle comes up over the thread. Take a small holding stitch at the top of the loop.

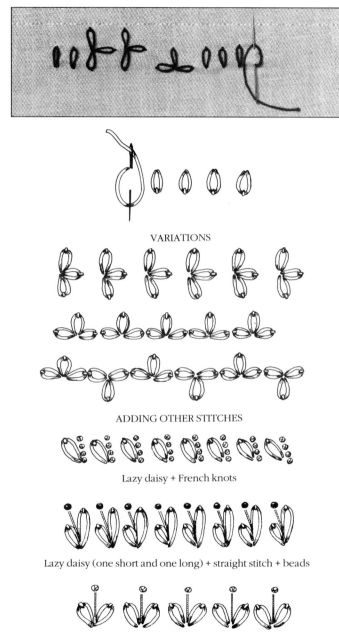

VARIATIONS

ADDING OTHER STITCHES

Lazy daisy + French knots

Lazy daisy (one short and one long) + straight stitch + beads

Lazy daisy + straight stitch + French knot or bead

Lazy daisy + French knot + straight stitch

MAGIC CHAIN STITCH

Thread the needle with two contrasting threads. Bring the needle up from the back and hold the threads with your thumb. Insert the needle at the starting point, so the threads form a loop. Bring the needle out a short distance away. Keep the light thread under the needle, and let the dark thread go above it (a). Pull the threads through. The light one will appear as a single chain stitch and the dark one will disappear behind the fabric. Repeat, this time holding the dark thread under the needle and the light one above (b). Continue on to make a chain, alternating light and dark (c).

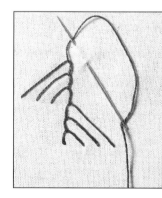

(a)   (b)   (c)

MAIDEN HAIR STITCH

Maiden hair stitch is a variation of the featherstitch and has a fernlike quality. Start exactly as for a featherstitch and work on equal sides of the seam. Work three single featherstitches on and to the left of the seam. Graduate the length of the stitches, making sure they line up vertically on the seam. Work a similar group to the right of the seam. Repeat.

OPEN CHAIN

Bring the needle up at A. Go back into the fabric a short distance to the right at B to form a loop. Bring the needle up directly below A at C (a). Keep the needle above the thread and pull gently to keep the loop shape. Repeat, inserting at B and pulling out at C, to make a continuous open chain

(b) (c). Remember, the needle is always slanted instead of straight as in a regular chain stitch.

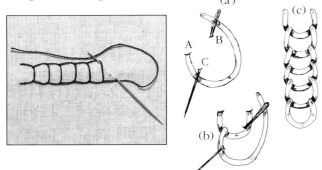

ROSE STITCH

This rose is loose and free-form. Start with a small cluster of French knots for the center (a). Along the sides, work stem stitch loosely in a circle (b). Form two or three rounds, letting the stitch grow larger with each round. Flatten out last round.

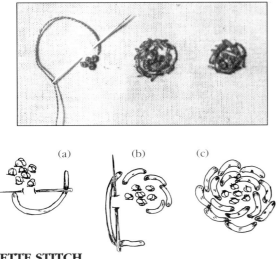

ROSETTE STITCH

Bring the thread up from the wrong side. Insert the needle close to thread and take a small stitch, leaving needle halfway through the stitch (a). Pull the thread up to the top and wrap or loop carefully three or four times (b). Try to keep the threads flat and lying side by side (c). Pull thread through and tack in place at both ends (d).

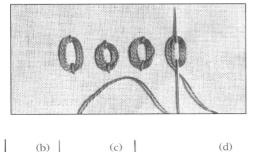

RUNNING STITCH

The running stitch is worked from right to left. Make small even stitches. The stitches that show should be the same length as the spaces.

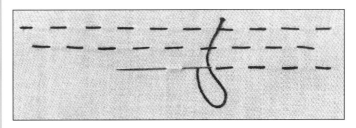

SATIN STITCH

Satin stitch was a favorite of Victorian crazy quilters. It can be worked in single or double layers to create a thick, smooth blanket of stitching. Lay down straight stitches close together, either straight up and down, side to side, or at an angle, to conform to the outlined shape.

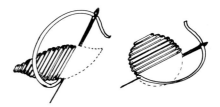

PHOTO DETAILS COURTESY DENVER ART MUSEUM

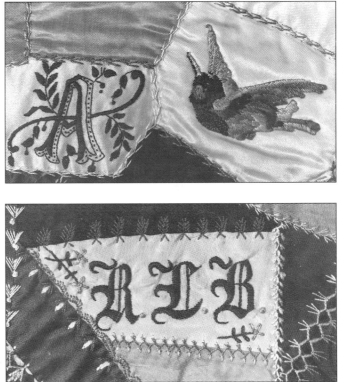

SCROLL STITCH

Work from left to right. The working thread is looped to the right and held in place with the left thumb. Take a small, slanted stitch in the center of the loop. Tighten the loop around the needle and pull the needle through.

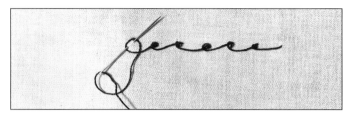

SHEAF STITCH

Sheaf stitch is a vertical tied stitch. With the needle, come up at A and go down at B. Come up to the right at C and go down at D. Come up at E and go down at F. Now, come up in the center, midway between C and D, and wrap the two outer threads, reinserting the needle at the center. Pull gently and go on to the next sheaf stitch.

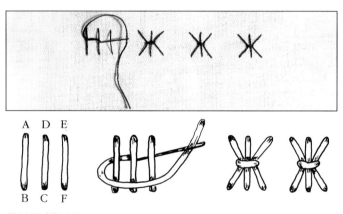

SNAIL TRAIL

Snail trail is worked from the right to travel along the seam line (a). Lay the thread flat along the line and hold with your thumb. Take a large, slanting stitch across the line from A to B. Twist the thread first over and then under the needle and pull through (b). The stitch can be altered by the slant of the needle and spacing.

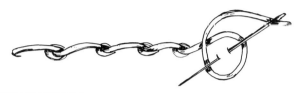

SPIDERS AND SPIDERWEBS

The spider and its web have appeared in fairy tales and Indian folklore and are found in every corner of the world. They were used in European needlework, and the Austrians considered them signs of good luck. It is no surprise to see them turn up in Victorian crazy quilts.

For spiderwebs, use metallic and iridescent threads that shimmer and shine. A good quality metallic thread is important for durability. I recommend the machine embroidery type. If you choose another type, use short lengths to prevent travelling. The spokes in the webs shown are couched down every ⅛" (3 mm) to ¼" (6 mm).

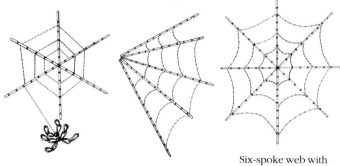

Four intersecting spokes   Corner web   Six-spoke web with continuous thread

Yes, spiders do have eight legs, four on each side! But it can be difficult to make them look nice. My compromise is to make them with six legs instead of eight. (My spider lost two legs when he was slammed in the screen door!) Each leg is made of two chain stitches connected to a body made of two iridescent beads. For those of you who can't compromise, here is one with eight legs.

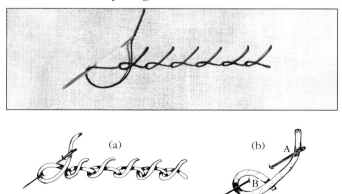

French knot

bead

single-strand silk twist

STEM STITCH

Stem stitch is worked from left to right. Sew along the stitch line and keep the thread to the left of the needle. Take small, even stitches. When using stem stitch to fill an area, be sure to fit lines snugly, side by side, in order to cover.

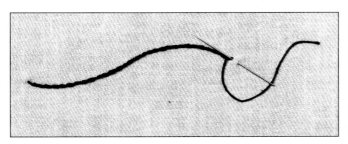

Photo Detail Courtesy Denver Art Museum

STRAIGHT STITCH

Straight stitches can be used in a variety of ways. Long or short, they should not be too loose, so pull threads firmly into place.

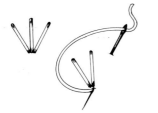

Trees, Shrubs, and Ground Cover

Crazy quilt landscapes can be enhanced with trees, shrubs, ground cover, and cactus that are embroidered with combination stitches. Each country has trees that are unique and typical to its region. Australia has the beautiful gum tree. Canada has the maple tree. Japan is home of the bonsai and cherry tree. The United States hosts the evergreen and the mighty oak.

Trunks of trees can be made with satin stitch or a combination of outline stitch and chain stitch. Lay these down side by side. Shade the trunk with a variety of colors (lights comes forward, darks recede). Leaves and small branches can be made with free-form featherstitching, maiden hair stitch, fly stitch, or cretan stitch. Punch needle embroidery with both thread and ribbon gives an excellent foliage effect. Work all other embroidery first to hold the layers together, then punch in the leaves or shrubbery.

Here are some stitching ideas for specific trees and plants:

BONSAI EVERGREEN

The rugged, twisted bonsai trunk is made of chain stitches laid side by side. The branches are free-form featherstitches. The needles are embroidered with medium-looped punch needle.

CACTUS

The many varieties of cactus can be worked in numerous ways. Try using punch needle or satin stitch. Lay stem stitches side by side. Add bead highlights for flowers.

CANADIAN MAPLE

The maple tree trunk is embroidered in outline stitch. The branches are free-form featherstitches. Leaves can be worked in smaller free-form featherstitches or medium-looped punch needle.

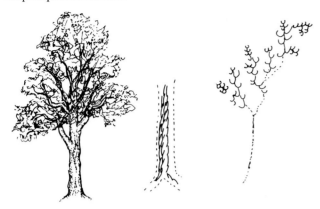

CHERRY TREE

The cherry tree, like many flowering trees—crabapple, apple, peach, crepe myrtle—is full and round. The trunk can be outlined with stem stitch and filled in with chain stitch. Leaves can be free-form featherstitches or punch needle. Add the flowers in the form of beads or ribbon punch needle.

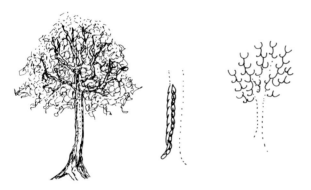

EVERGREEN

Rugged trunks are made with chain stitch and outline stitch laid side by side. The branches slope downward. Pine needles are embroidered with long-looped punch needle.

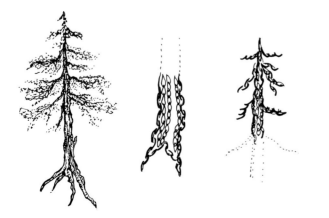

GUM TREE

One characteristic in common of the many gum tree varieties is that the leaves cluster up high at the end of long branches. Many types have unusual peeling trunks. The trunks can be embroidered with satin stitch; the leaves with punch needle.

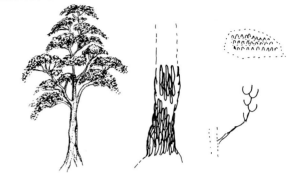

SHRUBBERY (e.g., SCRUB OAK, NANKING CHERRY)

Large shrubbery stems can be worked in chain stitch. Work stems in maiden hair stitches or featherstitches. Lay stitches on top of each other, using different shades for added depth. Come back in with punch needle embroidery and beading.

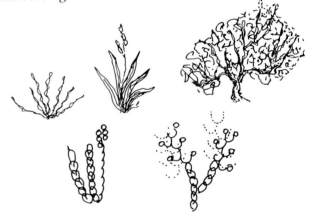

WEEPING WILLOW

The graceful weeping willow is worked with long and short satin stitches for the trunk and outline stitches for the long branches. The leaves are upside-down featherstitches.

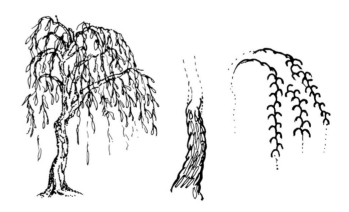

Findings

Crazy quilting is rather freewheeling. It follows very few rules yet encompasses a great many techniques. Here's a guide to the beads, laces, needles, and threads you may want to use in your work.

Left to right: Bugle, Ceylon, luster, metallic, metallic iris, seed, silver-lined rocaille, three-cut, translucent, transparent, transparent iris, two-cut. Far right, top to bottom: Pucha shell, turquoise, metal beads, Nymo thread, trade beads, crystal.

BEADS

Beads come in a wide range of sizes and shapes, and they span decades of time and miles of geography. From African trade beads to Austrian crystal to North American Indian pony beads to tiny seed beads, they can all be used in crazy quilting. Keep your beads well organized in see-through containers.

- **African trade**—A large colorful cylindrical bead used historically in Africa for trade.
- **Austrian crystal**—A lead glass crystal bead or drop in iridescent colors.
- **Bugle**—A longer-length bead, 2 mm across and ranging from 5 mm to 36 mm long! Can be ribbed, smooth, twisted, or faceted.
- **Ceylon**—A bead with a pearlized finish.
- **Luster opaque**—A low-sheen, solid bead.
- **Metallic**—A solid metallic bead. Gives off a rich sheen.
- **Metallic iris**—A bead with rich iridescence (e.g, bronze, gold, silver).
- **Pony**—A large, solid-color bead. Pony beads were used by North American Indians for trade.
- **Seed**—A tiny solid-color opaque bead. Typically used in Indian beadwork.
- **Silver-lined rocaille**—A glittery bead, clear with a silver-lined center. Very flashy.
- **Three-cut**—A bead with faceted sides and ends. Can be transparent, luster, silver-lined, satin, opaque metallic, color-lined, or luster opaque. Very flashy.

- **Translucent**—A bead that allows light through but is not transparent.
- **Transparent**—A see-through bead. Sometimes lined with a metallic or a color.
- **Transparent iris**—A bead with iridescent sheen.
- **Two-cut**—A bead with faceted sides and flat ends. Can be silver-lined, iris, satin, or opaque.

LACES

Lace is a delicate openwork fabric in which the threads form decorative designs. There are many different types.

- **Alençon**—Easily distinguishable by the heavy thread that outlines the design, usually a floral on a fine net background. Originally made by hand in Alençon, France.
- **Chantilly**—A very delicate lace featuring floral and scroll thread outlines on a mesh background. Originally made in Chantilly, France.

Top to bottom: Alençon, Chantilly, Cluny, motifs, tatting, Teneriffe, Val, Venice.

design. The background is eliminated in the finishing process.

♦ **Lace yardage**—Extra-wide lace or lace yardage can be used as an overlay in crazy quilting. Be sure that the overlay is light enough to let the fabric color show through. Lay the lace over the fabric, cut the two pieces as one, and sew into the foundation. Lay the wide lace piece into a corner for added textures or to soften an area.

NEEDLES

There is nothing more frustrating than not having the proper needle for a sewing task. Try to keep a full range of sizes and types in your needlecase.

♦ **Beading**—A long, fine needle with a thin eye. Used strictly for beading.

♦ **Between**—Much like a sharp, but shorter. Usually used in quilting or hand sewing.

♦ **Chenille**—A large-eyed needle that will take heavy yarns. Used in ribbon embroidery.

♦ **Crewel**—A sharp needle with a long eye. Excellent for ribbon embroidery. Comes in many sizes.

♦ **Darner**—A long needle with a large eye. Used for darning wool. Good for heavy ribbon work and twisted yarns.

♦ **Sharp**—A small-eyed, fine needle. Used with sewing threads and to attach single beads.

♦ **Cluny**—A coarse crochet type lace made of heavy cotton thread and characterized by wheel or paddle designs. Named for the Cluny Museum in France.

♦ **Motifs**—Individual lace medallions that can be purchased singly or clipped apart from larger lace pieces.

♦ **Point d'espirit**—A net lace with dots covering the entire piece.

♦ **Tatting lace**—A lace of a tiny little circles in a row that imitate old-fashioned tatting.

♦ **Teneriffe**—A patterned lace that looks like little cobwebs or wheels. Originally designed in Teneriffe, France.

♦ **Val**—A narrow lace with a net background that has either round or diamond-shaped holes. The woven design is flat, sheer, and usually flowered. Originated in Valenciennes, France.

♦ **Venice**—This lace looks like joined flowers. A multitude of close stitches creates a heavy

Left to right: Beading, between, chenille, crewel, darner, sharp, straw, tapestry.

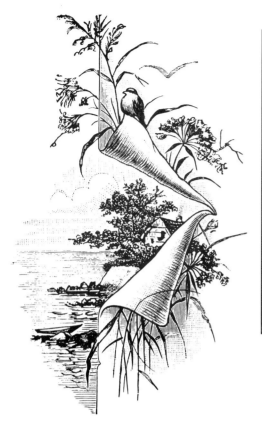

Clockwise, from top left: Brazilian embroidery thread, crewel yarn, metallics, Natesh, tapestry wool, embroidery floss, silk sewing thread, silk ribbon, silk buttonhole twist, Persian wool, pearl cotton.

✦ **Straw**—A long, narrow milliner's needle, the same thickness from end to end. Excellent for making French knots.

✦ **Tapestry**—A blunt needle with a large eye. Used for cross-stitch and needlepoint.

THREADS

Don't be afraid to use a variety of threads in your crazy quilting. Collect as many threads as possible, and keep them out where you can see them. I use plastic bags arranged on rings and hang them from wall hooks. I store spools and carded threads in hardware drawers with clear plastic fronts (the kind usually used for nuts and bolts). Refer to the Source Guide for companies that mail-order threads.

✦ **Brazilian embroidery thread**—A rayon twisted embroidery thread. Use short lengths as it tends to knot up. Some people suggest running it across a damp washcloth before using to eliminate the kinks.

✦ **Crewel yarn**—A very fine three-stranded wool. The strands can be separated and used singly for embroidery.

✦ **Metallics**—Any thread with a glitter or shine. There are many metallics on the market. Keep a good variety on hand for couching and weaving techniques. I prefer machine embroidery metallics because they are smoother and pass through fabric easily. Look for variegated threads such as Astro by Madeira.

✦ **Natesh**—A rayon thread with a wonderful sheen. Double it for Victorian stitching. It's also good for machine embroidery.

✦ **Pearl cotton**—A rather thick, twisted thread with low luster that is often used for crochet. It's wonderful in embroidery for creating texture. Available in sizes 3, 5, and 8 (the thinnest).

✦ **Persian wool**—A three-stranded wool, thicker than crewel but thinner than tapestry, that can be easily separated. Use it for textural work in pictorial crazy quilting.

✦ **Silk buttonhole twist**—An exquisite thread that will surely spoil you! The silk takes on a special sheen that stands up to lots of wear—plus it feeds through the fabric so easily! I use it exclusively for Victorian stitches. One strand is equivalent to three strands of embroidery floss. For a two hundred-plus color range, try Kanagawa silk threads.

✦ **Silk ribbon**—A dream to work with! Silk ribbon can be used in a variety of ways, including embroidery, punch needle, and covering seams. It creates wonderful texture and is very pliable and soft. Comes in 2 mm, 4 mm, and 9 mm widths.

✦ **Silk sewing thread**—A thread often used for machine embroidery. Try combining it with other threads.

✦ **Stranded embroidery floss**—A six-stranded cotton that can be used one strand at a time or in multiples. For Victorian stitches, use two or three strands. Comes in a wide color range.

✦ **Tapestry wool**—A thick, bulky yarn traditionally used for needlepoint. It can be used in punch needle or embroidery. Try combining it with metallics.

International Terms and Measurements

I have discovered in my travels that different countries use different words for similar products. Australia, Canada, and the United States may speak the same language, but believe me, we mean different things! In addition, Canada, Japan, and Australia are on the metric system, which makes for difficulty in sizing patterns. Here are tables of terms and measurements that I hope will simplify it all for you.

TERMS

United States (term + definition)	Australia	Canada	Japan
Art board—A very strong, heavy compressed cardboard, e.g., Crescent board.	art board	artist board	kosaku yo atsu-gami
Batting—A fluffy cotton or polyester bonded filler. Used as interlining between quilt top and backing. Comes in various thicknesses.	wadding	batting or wadding	kiruto-wata
Calico fabric—Cotton fabric, usually with small, overall floral print.	patchwork cotton	calico	kobana-print cotton
Embroidery floss—Six-strand embroidery cotton.	embroidery cotton	floss	shisyu-ito
Fleece—A thick dense batting used in clothing and craft construction, e.g., Pellon fleece, needlepunch fleece.	rayfelt	Thermolam®	ashuku-men
Iron-on interfacing—A stiffening material that can be bonded to the back of fabric using a hot iron.	Vylene® iron-on interfacing	fusible interfacing	chingi
Matt board—Colored board used for the inner framing of paintings and prints.	mount	matt	kami-matto
Muslin—A cream-colored cotton fabric.	calico	muslin	kinari-men
Spray starch—A sizing, sprayed from a can, that adds body and stiffness to fabric.	sizing	spray starch	spray-nori

APPROXIMATE EQUIVALENT MEASUREMENTS

INCHES	CENTIMETERS		YARDS	METERS
1"	2.5 cm		1 yard	.91 meter
2"	5 cm		2 yards	1.83 meters
3"	8 cm			
4"	10 cm		**COMMON MEASUREMENTS**	
5"	13 cm		1/16"	1.5 mm
12"	30 cm		1/8"	3.0 mm
			1/4"	6.0 mm
			1/2"	12 mm
FEET	**METERS**		3/4"	18 mm
1'	.30 meter			
2'	.61 meter			
3'	.91 meter			

Source Guide

The following are reputable businesses that I deal with personally.
SASE = self-addressed stamped envelope
SI = Ships Internationally

Australia

Anne's Glory Box
60-62 Beaumont Street
Hamilton, New South Wales, 2303, Australia
*Complete line of quilting and embroidery supplies,
laces, books, and many more needlework supplies.
Retail and wholesale. Send business-size SASE. SI.*

Ruth's Patchwork Supplies
43 Gloucester Street
High Gate Hill
Brisbane, Queensland, 4101, Australia
*Patchwork supplies and quarterly newsletter featur-
ing latest fabrics and samples–each newsletter
includes fifteen (4"× 8") fabrics and a gift item.
Australian membership, $30.00. For mail-order, send
SASE. SI.*

Canada

Cloth Shop
4515 West 105th Avenue
Vancouver, British Columbia
Canada V6R 2H8
32-page color catalog, $3.00. SI.

Quilter's Helper
Box 519
5511 Main Street
Osgoode, Ontario
Canada K0A 2W0
*Specialized cottons for quilting and home decorat-
ing; also books and supplies. Catalog and fabric
swatches, $3.00. SI.*

Silver Thimble Inc.
64 Rebecca, Dept. cq
Oakville, Ontario
Canada, L6K IJ2

Japan
Yama Quilt Stores
1-S-3 Kichi-jogi Minamicho
Musashino City
Tokyo, Japan
A bit of American quilting in Tokyo. Fully supplied with all the latest in quilting materials and supplies.

United States
☞ GENERAL
Aardvark Adventures in Handcrafts
P.O. Box 2449, Dept. cq
Livermore, CA 94550
U.S.A.
Stamps, buttons, a wide variety of threads and supplies. Publishes a marvelous newspaper/catalog. Send two first-class stamps and return address.

Judith Designs
P.O. Box 177
Castle Rock, CO 80104
U.S.A.
Findings from around the world for crazy quilting and clothing embellishment. Doodads, fabric kits, beads, buttons, silk thread, ribbons. Catalog, $1.50. SI.

Kasuri Dyeworks
1959 Shattuck Avenue
Berkeley, CA 94704
U.S.A.
Japanese fabrics, threads, charms, dye supplies, books. Catalog, $5.00. SI

Ragtime/An Eclectic Collection
515 Wilcox
Castle Rock, CO 80104
U.S.A.
Vintage clothing, antique laces, and collecitbles. Inquire for specific items.

☞ BEADS, BUTTONS, AND DOODADS
Eagle Feather Trading Post
168 West 12th Street
Ogden, UT 84404
U.S.A.
Beadwork supplies. Catalog, $3.00.

The Freed Company
415 Central N.W.
Box 394
Albuquerque, NM 87103
U.S.A.
Unusual beads and fetishes. A wonderful trading post atmosphere. Send SASE for catalog.

Garden of Beadin'
Box 1535
Redway, CA 95560
U.S.A.
Beads and beading supplies. Catalog, $2.00.

The Handswork
P.O. Box 386
Pecos, NM 87552
U.S.A.
Handmade and handpainted machine-washable buttons. Catalog, $2.00 (refundable with first order). SI.

Shipwreck Beads
5021 Mud Bay Road
Olympia, WA 98502
U.S.A.
Over 2,000 beads! Color catalog, $3.00.

Small Wonders
1317 S.E. Blvd.
Spokane, WA 99202
U.S.A.
Sterling and 14K gold charms and thimble cages. Send SASE. SI.

Western Trading Post
P.O. Box 9070
Denver, CO 80209-0070
U.S.A.
Wholesale and retail beads, tools, feathers, aluminum dance cones. Catalog, $3.00.

☞ EMBROIDERY
Y. L. I.
P. O. Box 109
Provo, UT 84601
U.S.A.
Needlework supplies. Carries Kanagawa silk ribbon and threads [Judith uses these exclusively in her work]. Retail and wholesale catalog, $1.50. SI.

Things Japanese
9805 N.E. 116th Street, Suite 7160
Kirkland, WA 98034
U.S.A.

Japanese silk filament, ribbon, thread. Catalog and swatches, $4.00. SI.

Treadleart
25834 Narbonne Avenue
Lomita, CA 90717
U.S.A.

☞ FABRICS AND DYES
Cerulean Blue
P.O. Box 21168
Seattle, WA 98111–3168
U.S.A.
All types of supplies for the dyer and painter of fabric. Color catalog, $4.50.

Shades
2880 Holcomb Br. Road
Box 9, Dept. cq
Alpharetta, GA 30201
U.S.A.
Dyed cottons and silks by the yard. Catalog, $5.00.

Thai Silks
252 State Street, Dept. cq
Modesto, CA 94022
U.S.A.
The largest selection of silk materials—very reasonable. Send SASE for catalog information. SI.

Yvonne Porcella Studios
3619 ShoemakerAvenue
Modesto, CA 95351
U.S.A.
Books and patterns. Dyed fabrics by order only. Commissions accepted. Send SASE for catalog. SI.

☞ FRAMES AND BOXES
Tennessee Wood Crafters
P.O. Box 239
Springfield, TN 37172
U.S.A.
Wood boxes, frames, decorative wood items for needlework insertion. Send SASE for catalog. SI.

☞ LACE
Heirlooms by Emily
R.D.#1, Box 190
Glen Rock, PA 17327
U.S.A.
Laces, swiss batiste, inserts, borders. Catalog, $2.50.

☞ PATTERNS
Folkwear Patterns
Customer Service, Dept. cq
The Taunton Press

Box 5506
Newtown, CT 06470-5506
U.S.A.
Authentic ethnic and historical garment patterns. Catalog, $2.00 (check or money order).

☞ PHOTOGRAPHY
Grandma Graphics
Dept. BCQ 20 Birling Gap
Fairport, NY 14450-3916
U.S.A.
Photo sun print kits. Send SASE for free price list. SI.

☞ PUNCH NEEDLE
Bernadine's/Igolochkoy
411 Crestwood Drive
Arthur, IL 61911
U.S.A.
Punch needles, supplies, patterns, kits, threads, yarns. Catalog, $2.00 (refundable with first order). SI.

Clarks O Sew Easy Punch Embroidery
252 Vega Drive
Goleta, CA 93117
U.S.A.
Punch needles, patterns, kits, yarn for all punch embroidery. Retail and wholesale catalog. SI.

Marinda Stewart
P.O. Box 402, Dept. J
Walnut Creek, CA 94596
U.S.A.
Punch needle book, clothing patterns, fabric packs. Send SASE.

☞ TOOLS
Anne Powell Ltd.
P.O. Box 3060
Stuart, FL 34995
U.S.A.
Fine needlework tools and supplies, antique tools, books. Catalog, $2.00.

Clotilde Inc.
237 S.W. 28th Street
Fort Lauderdale, FL 33315
U.S.A.
Every type of sewing aid imaginable. Catalog, $2.00.

Lacis
2982 Adeline Street, Dept JM
Berkeley, CA 99703
U.S.A.
Lacemaking tools, heirloom sewing supplies, books, needlework tools. Catalog, $1.00.

Bibliography

Aikman, Susanne Z. *A Primer: The Art of Native American Beadwork.* Denver: Morning Flower Press, 1980.

Barton, Julia. *The Art of Embroidery.* London: Merehurst Press, 1989.

Bond, Dorothy. *Crazy Quilt Stitches.* Cottage Grove, Oreg., 1981.

Bradford, Jenny. *Silk Ribbon Embroidery: Australian Wildflower Designs.* Ellwood, Victoria, Australia: Greenhouse Publications, 1988.

————.*Silk Ribbon Embroidery II: Transform Your Clothes.* Ellwood, Victoria, Australia: Greenhouse Publications, 1989.

————.*Silk Ribbon Embroidery III: For Gifts and Garments.* Birchgrove, New South Wales, Australia: Publishing Printing Ltd, 1990.

Brown-Stewart, Marinda. *Ideas and Inspirations: A Punch Needle Technique Primer.* El Cerrito, Calif., 1983.

Carroll, Mary. *Making Needlecraft Landscapes.* New York: St. Martins Press, 1986.

Coats and Clark. *100 Embroidery Stitches.* New York: Coats and Clark, 1964.

Darling Kindersley Ltd. *The Pattern Library, Embroidery.* New York: Ballentine Books, 1981.

Elsworth, Wendy. "Beading on Leather." *Threads Magazine* 7 (October/November 1986), 50-53.

Erickson, Lois, and Diane Erickson. *Ethnic Costumes.* New York: Van Nostrand Reinholdt Company, 1979.

Groves, Sylvia. *The History of Needlework Tools and Accessories.* New York: Arco Press, 1973.

Joynes, Heather. *Ribbon Embroidery.* Kenthurst, Australia: Kangaroo Press, 1988.

Kennedy, Jill, and Jane Varrall. *Painting on Silk.* London: Dryard Press Ltd., 1988.

Korach, Alice. "Bead Knitting Madness." *Threads Magazine* 24 (August/September 1989), 24-29.

Leffingwell, Jeanne. "A Thousand Points of Light." *Threads Magazine* 30 (August/September 1990), 38-42.

Lyford, Carrie A. *Quill and Beadwork of the Western Sioux.* Boulder, Colo.: Johnson Publishing Co.,1979.

Mailes, Thomas E. *The Pueblo Children of the Earth Mother.* 2 vols. Garden City, N.Y.: Doubleday & Company, 1983.

McMorris, Penny. *Crazy Quilts.* New York: E. P. Dutton, 1984.

Meilach, Dona Z., and Dee Menagh. *Exotic Needlework.* New York: Crown Publishers Inc.,1978.

Nichols, Marion. *Encyclopedia of Embroidery Stitches, Including Crewel.* New York: Dover Publications, 1974.

Peterson, Greta. *Stitches and Decorative Seams.* New York: Van Nostrand Reinholdt Company, 1983.

Porcella, Yvonne. *A Colorful Book.* Modesto, Calif.: Porcella Studios, 1987.

Rolfe, Margaret. *Patchwork Quilts in Australia.* Richmond, Victoria, Australia: Greenhouse Publications,1987.

Swan-Burrows, Susan. *A Winterthur Guide to American Needlework.* New York: Crown Publishers Inc.,1976.

Thomas, Mary. *Mary Thomas's Dictionary of Embroidery Stitches.* New York: Crescent Books, 1989.

Thompson, Sue. *Decorative Dressmaking.* Emmaus, Pa.: Rodale Press, 1985

Wilson, Erica. *Crewel Embroidery.* New York: Charles Scribner's Sons, 1982.

————.*The Craft of Silk and Gold Thread Embroidery and Stumpwork.* New York: Charles Scribner's Sons, 1973.

————.*Erica Wilson's Embroidery Book.* New York: Charles Scribner's Sons, 1973.

About the Author

PHOTO:
ALLEN CARTER

J udith Montano is a Canadian artist who grew up on the Bar U Ranch in the foothills of Alberta. The many influences of her childhood can be seen in her work today. The neighboring Stoney Indian reserve provided many playmates as well as teachers. The Hutterite colony to the east gave her a background in sewing and needlework. Her mother was a great influence, and taught her needlework of many types at an early age. An isolated ranch life encouraged a sense of independence and an active imagination. High school years were spent in the city with her godparents, who taught her to value tradition and culture. Judith later attended the University of California at Chico, where she received a B.A. in fine arts and journalism. Upon graduating, she painted with the San Francisco Art Guild for one year.

Over the next seven years, Judith lived in England, Japan, and Germany and traveled extensively. Each country provided a wealth of design and inspiration. Oil painting and artwork had to be modified with the arrival of her son, Jason, and daughter, Madeleine. Before long, she discovered quilting and fiber arts.

Settling for seven years in Humble, Texas, she opened a British antique shop with a European tearoom. Wearing many hats, Judith was chef, antique dealer, and waitress, and she carried a small landscape design business on the side. Judith became a charter member of the Kingwood Quilt Guild and served as president and publicity chairman. Through this avenue, she met many quilt artists and teachers and became interested in crazy quilting and art-to-wear garments.

Crazy quilting is the traditional base for all of Judith's contemporary accessories and garments. After working with traditional quilting and winning several national awards, she turned to the free form of crazy quilting, which proved to be an outlet

Three Sisters, Alberta, Canada

Three Sisters, Katoomba Blue Mountains, Australia

for her love of vibrant color, lush fabrics, and embellishments.

Judith lectures and teaches throughout Canada, the United States, Australia, and Japan. Her designs and articles have appeared in *American Home Arts, Better Homes and Gardens, Craft Art, Creative Ideas for Living, Lady's Circle Patchwork Quilts, Needle and Thread, Needle Craft, Needlecraft for Today, Quilter's Newsletter Magazine, Quilting Today, Quilting U.S.A., Quilts Down Under, Quilts Japan,* and *Sew News.* Her work has been displayed at the Denver Art Museum, and many of her creations are in museum collections. Her art garments have been shown internationally through the Denver Art Museum, the Fairfield/Concord Fashion Show, and the Kanagawa Thread Company, Tokyo, Japan. In addition, she has been featured in many art-to-wear shows, among them "Accessories as Art," Houston, Texas; "Arapahoe Art-to-Wear," Denver, Colorado; "Art-to-Wear," Paducah, Kentucky; "Cut from the Same Cloth" sponsored by Concord Fabrics; "The Dairy Barn," Athens, Ohio; "Profiles," Edmonton,

Alberta, Canada; and "Quilts Colorado," Mitskoshi Department Store, Tokyo, Japan. Judith has been featured as the guest artist at the Melbourne Trade Show in Australia, the "Profiles" show in Canada, and the Tokyo Hobby Show in Japan. She has made guest appearances on many television shows, including "Good Morning Australia" and "The Today Show" in Australia.

Judith's current work concentrates on contemporary art pieces with an Indian theme, using crazy quilting and other needlework techniques. Long-range goals include a video on crazy quilt techniques and a book on her journey into self-help and awareness that deals with her Indian beliefs and encounters in Japan and Australia.

Judith resides three-quarters of the year in Castle Rock, Colorado, and one-quarter in Gosford, New South Wales, Australia. For further information on Judith's workshops and lectures, write to:

Judith Designs
P.O. Box 177
Castle Rock, CO 80104

Other Fine Quilting Books
from C & T Publishing

A Celebration of Hearts, Jean Wells and Marina Anderson

An Amish Adventure, Roberta Horton

Baltimore Album Quilts, Historic Notes and Antique Patterns, Elly Sienkiewicz

Baltimore Beauties and Beyond, Volume I, Elly Sienkiewicz

Baltimore Beauties and Beyond, Volume II, Elly Sienkiewicz

Boston Commons Quilt, Blanche Young and Helen Young Frost

Calico and Beyond, Roberta Horton

Crazy Quilt Handbook, Judith Montano

Crosspatch, Pepper Cory

Diamond Patchwork, Jeffrey Gutcheon

Fans, Jean Wells

Fine Feathers, Marianne Fons

Flying Geese Quilt, Blanche Young and Helen Young Frost

Friendship's Offering, Susan McKelvey

Heirloom Machine Quilting, Harriet Hargrave

Irish Chain Quilt, Blanche Young and Helen Young Frost

Landscapes and Illusions, Joen Wolfrom

Let's Make Waves, Marianne Fons and Liz Porter

Light and Shadows, Susan McKelvey

Mandala, Katie Pasquini

Mariner's Compass, Judy Mathieson

New Lone Star Handbook, Blanche Young and Helen Young Frost

Perfect Pineapples, Jane Hall and Dixie Haywood

Picture This, Jean Wells and Marina Anderson

Plaids and Stripes, Roberta Horton

Quilting Designs From the Amish, Pepper Cory

Quilting Designs From Antique Quilts, Pepper Cory

Radiant Nine Patch, Blanche Young

Stained Glass Quilting Technique, Roberta Horton

Trip Around the World Quilts, Blanche Young and Helen Young Frost

Visions: Quilts of a New Decade, Quilt San Diego

Working in Miniature, Becky Schaefer

Wearable Art For Real People, Mary Mashuta

3 Dimensional Design, Katie Pasquini

For more information, write for a free catalog from

C & T Publishing
P.O. Box 1456
Lafayette, CA 94553